GLOUCESTER MASSACHUSETTS

THE **ORGANIZED** HOME

DESIGN SOLUTIONS FOR CLUTTER-FREE LIVING

QUARRY BOOKS

Randall Koll and Casey Ellis

First published in the United States of America by
Quarry Books, an imprint of
Rockport Publishers, Inc.
33 Commercial Street
Gloucester, Massachusetts 01930-5089
Telephone: (978) 282-9590
Fax: (978) 283-2742
www.rockpub.com

Library of Congress Cataloging-in-Publication Data
Koll, Randall.
   The organized home : design solutions for clutter-free living / Randall Koll and Casey Ellis.
      p.   cm.
   ISBN 1-59253-018-4
   1. Interior decoration. 2. Storage in the home. I. Ellis, Casey. II. Title.
NK2115.K63 2004
747—dc22

2003020900
CIP

ISBN 1-59253-018-4

10 9 8 7 6 5 4 3 2 1

Design: Yee Design
Cover Image: Eric Roth/Beverly Rivkind Design
Back Cover: (from left to right) Courtesy of McGuire Furniture Company; Courtesy of Roche Bobois;
   Courtesy of the Kohler Company
Spine: Courtesy of Maine Cottage Furniture

Printed in China

To our mothers, Ollie Jones and Kathy Suesens.

contents

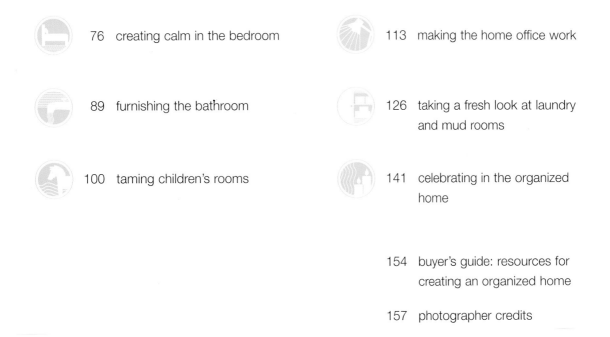

organizing by design

The organized home is a home that works, a place where bookshelves are orderly rather than overflowing, closet doors do not conceal chaos, and frantic searches for car keys are rare. If this isn't your home, it could be.

Our philosophy is that furniture and accessories should increase storage capacity and control clutter while adding to the overall design aesthetic. Choose your furniture wisely and then let it do the work. But choose it as an interior designer would, with equal emphasis on good looks and efficient function for your specific needs. Whether you are embarking on a major change of decor or simply want to rearrange the furniture you have to gain a fresh look and maximize storage, the ideas in this book will help you reach your goals.

How to begin? With an honest look at your lifestyle and a realistic appraisal of your budget. After that, look at your rooms without slipping into tired design stereotypes. A dining room table does not have to sit in the center of the room just because that's where most people place it. Putting it in a corner, next to a built-in banquette, could free enough space to incorporate a bookcase and a comfortable chair or two. It's easy to contemplate using an extra bedroom as an office, but it may be harder to imagine the dining room doubling as a library. Yet, wouldn't you use the space more if it held some of your favorite books and an attractive nook for reading them in?

Every room in the house can benefit from creative thinking. Why not give a chaise lounge from a consignment store a new terry cloth slipcover and a spot in your bathroom? You'll add an instant touch of spalike luxury. Need more storage space in your home office? Set a pair of multidrawer architectural flat files in the middle of the room to create a hard-working island, a design concept too good to confine to the kitchen. If there's a vintage tea cart gathering dust in the basement, bring it upstairs, give it a fresh coat of paint, and use it as a table for your laptop computer. Move it next to your desk for some tasks, and then roll it alongside an easy chair for others.

How do you find all these ingredients for great makeovers? You shop. But you shop as a design professional would when he or she augments purchases from to-the-trade-only showrooms. Welcome to the wonderful world of creative design shopping, which runs the gamut of sources from antique stores, consignment shops, and flea markets to salvage yards, office supply stores, and even your own home. Where, in fact, some of the most satisfying "shopping" can occur: not only for pieces from the attic, basement, or garage to revamp, but also for furniture to move from one room to another where it might function better.

There are no hard and fast rules in this book, although there are some freely admitted prejudices and crotchets, including dismay at the failure of so many homeowners to do much living in their living rooms and exasperation at the over-abundance of unused toys in most children's rooms. Unlike many other books on organization, this one does not preach that clutter control is simply a matter of hardening your heart, gathering up a clutch of garbage bags, and throwing away piles of possessions based on arbitrary guidelines. We wouldn't dream of declaring that you must discard clothes you haven't worn in a year or that you should stop buying artwork because you are running out of wall space. Who are we to say how many pairs of shoes or signed lithographs you should own? We only ask you to open your eyes, evaluate the way your home does or doesn't work now, and consider some offbeat, even quirky, uses of furniture and accessories to make it both better organized and more attractive.

Once you reach that happy state, you need to address maintenance. We've found that if family members incorporate simple rituals and positive habits into their lives, maintaining organized rooms becomes relatively easy. One of the most valuable aids to maintenance is the keeping of a household journal. This is where you note what you need, what you yearn for, what works, and what doesn't. It need not be a massive, vellum-bound reminiscent of a volume in the library of a stately English home; it doesn't even have to be a book. Allocate a file on your computer for your journal entries if that works better for you.

Finally, we've suggested some seasonal changes for most rooms, small ways to acknowledge that an organized home is always evolving, changing as our lives change, staying in tune with the pleasures and challenges of the passing years.

creating a first impression

How do you make an entrance great? And, more importantly, how do you make it organized? Planning is the key. As with any space that sees a lot of traffic, clutter can quickly transform an entryway into a bastion of disorder. When organized, however, the space will serve you and your guests well. Functional furniture, a pleasing array of art objects, and simple fresh flowers or plants will create a warmly welcoming introduction to your home.

Think of the entryway as less of a hall and more of a room. How would you need to furnish a room with a lot of activity? First, plenty of places for coats and bags—say an armoire or a well-outfitted closet. Next, surfaces clear of clutter not only make a good first impression but also provide a place to set things like a guest book or name tags for a child's birthday party.

Entryways should facilitate flow, including the flow of items that are set down—like shopping bags and gifts—and things meant to be hung up—like coats, purses, and hats. If there isn't an available surface, hook, or hanger, these items end up hanging on a doorknob, tossed over a banister, or just dropped in a pile.

Just as the entryway deserves organizational attention, so too do the other hallways in the house. They also offer interesting opportunities for additional storage and for displaying collectibles. Long hallways can provide marvelous book storage or display many types of art, but it's also useful to rethink small hall spaces. Where a hall ends is not necessarily the end of useful space. Put a chair and a revolving bookstand there to create a reading nook, or install a bookcase under a window.

You can even tuck a mini-workplace into a hallway. The corner where two hallways meet or the end of a hallway—especially one with a window—can hold a narrow desk and slim chair. Define the area by painting the section of wall behind the desk a different color and hanging a distinctive piece of artwork or a good-looking bulletin board. Even the shortest, narrowest hall can hold a little something useful, such as a small bookcase or an old oak student's chair with a desklike arm.

OPPOSITE *An eye-catching primitive hatstand adds decorative flair to an entrance, while providing a natural spot to store hats, umbrellas, and walking sticks. A small bench handles the overflow and creates convenient seating.*

Functional Furniture

At first glance entryways and halls may appear to need little in the way of organization and storage capacity. Rethinking these spaces as rooms rather than mere passageways, however, will reveal the usefulness of including practical furniture pieces. Think outside the box, and search out something a bit quirky or unusual: perhaps a buffet or breakfront that would usually grace a dining room, a primitive pie safe with pierced tin inserts, or even an old church pew. Remember: the rule is to furnish the hall, not overfill it with furniture. Furniture choices should serve the activity of the hall, not just stand idle as decorative pieces.

Mirrors. Always have a mirror in an entrance hall. It creates a place for guests to check their appearance upon arrival and a last chance for you to check yours before departing.

Seating. Chairs, benches, and stools all can work well here, depending on the size of the space and your decor. Benches with lift-up seats provide both seating and storage. A stool in the entryway of a home with a "shoes off" policy makes it unnecessary for guests to balance on one leg like a flamingo while removing their shoes. But don't fill the entryway with seating. This is a transient place; keep the flow open.

Umbrella Holders and Hatstands. A must for areas with months of wet weather, an umbrella holder or hatstand also offers a way to introduce an interesting accent piece to the space year round. Antique collectives stock an array of quirky stands, from deep majolica cylinders for umbrellas and walking sticks to ornate Victorian-era pieces that also hold hats and coats. Even a massive terra-cotta garden urn can hold umbrellas. Keep extras on hand for visitors who arrive in good weather and must depart in bad. Supplement water-repellant umbrellas with Chinese paper parasols for sun protection on walks and antique walking sticks for hikes.

Armoires. If you have room in the entryway for an armoire it can double your entry closet space, add a hidden storage area, and conceal stereo equipment, a fax machine, or an extension phone. An armoire with a mirrored door will double the look of your space and add architectural interest.

Sideboards. Originally designed for dining rooms, sideboards function well in entries. Their generous surface can hold a handsome basket, lacquer box, or wooden bowl to store keys, as well as provide space for a plant or flower arrangement. Just don't let the drawers become catchalls. Reserve them for items you need to find quickly when you're about to leave the house. Designate their contents: local maps in one, for instance, camera film in another, driving or gym gloves in a third. Don't mix and match. "Miscellaneous" drawers are the bane of an organized home.

Tables. In narrow entryways, altar tables or console tables give you a long surface space without taking up much depth. Stack interesting old wooden boxes, such as map cases, Chinese wedding chests, and small tansu (Japanese storage pieces) underneath to create a decorative still life that provides plenty of storage space.

A central table can bring a large entryway down to more human proportions. This could be a library table, an inherited dining table with the extension leaves removed, or even an old pine table that doesn't fit in the kitchen. All provide a generous amount of usable surface space. Those

OPPOSITE *A kitchen sideboard, moved to the entrance, makes an elegant statement of sweeping surface space for over-sized floral arrangements and unusual collectibles. Roomy drawers keep keys, maps, sunglasses, and gloves out-of-sight but within easy reach.*

A FORMULA FOR EASY ENTRIES

Furnishing an entryway effectively can be as simple as combining three easy-to-find pieces:

- A large mirror, a table with a slim drawer, and a stool stored underneath;

- A painted bench, an umbrella stand, and a cluster of oversized wall hooks;

- A Japanese tansu, a small stool, and a tall basket filled with twisted willow branches;

- A pine dresser flanked by a painted metal garden chair on one side and an antique hatstand on the other;

- An extra dining room chair set alongside a skirted table holding a generously proportioned lamp with a hand-painted shade.

with drawers under the top for concealed storage are even better. A gateleg table, with its two folding leaves, is a versatile possibility.

Dressers. Low dressers designed for bedrooms combine tablelike surface space with the valuable storage of drawers. A highboy provides extensive drawer space, while making a strong decorative statement with its height and scale.

Étagères and Baker's Racks. Ideally suited for smaller entryways, these take up less visual space than solid furniture pieces. The open shelving can hold interesting baskets and boxes to increase their storage capacity.

An Open-Topped Wooden Box or Large Basket for the Closet. The typical entryway closet is fitted with a single clothing rod beneath a shelf, but this may not be the most efficient use of the space. Consider removing the rod and mounting large, two-pronged hooks along the back closet wall. This frees floor space at the front for a low storage piece.

Book Storage Galore

Hallways can provide considerable book storage. If your hallways are narrow, forget standard twelve-inch (30 cm deep) bookshelves; many books will fit comfortably on shelves as little as seven inches (18 cm) deep. For a wider hallway, line one wall with bookshelves and place a narrow table holding a lamp on the other. A comfortable chair alongside the table would be a welcome addition.

A stairwell can be an unexpected but effective place to house books. If the area is wide enough, installing seven- to nine-inch (18 to 23 cm deep) shelves along one wall will create generous book storage space as well as places to display collectibles. Add light strips under the shelves and track lighting on the ceiling to highlight the display areas and make finding a book easier.

TOP *A chest of drawers, either new or antique, can be home to telephone directories, seasonal accessories, binoculars, or camera equipment. A pedestal plate of green apples paired with a long-blooming orchid plant are easy seasonal additions.*

BOTTOM *A bookshelf-lined hallway allows family and guests to choose from a multitude of titles. Tucking additional shelves under a staircase makes use of space often wasted.*

Closets under stairways often become clutter catchers. Removing the door and converting the space to bookshelves creates a far more accessible storage space.

Even a single bookshelf hung in a small section of a hallway can be both useful and attractive. Look in salvage shops for interesting pieces of cornice or exterior trim once used around windows and doors. Add old iron or wooden brackets underneath to turn them into shelves.

The Hallway as Gallery

A hallway can be an ideal place to showcase art. Drawings, prints, small paintings—pieces you enjoy more by viewing them up close—work best. But before hanging a single artwork, approach the area as a gallery owner would and install first-rate lighting. It will make a tremendous difference.

Next, consider the arrangement of the art. Hanging a large group of paintings single-file down the length of a hall limits your ability to add works later. Instead, arrange them in clusters, which will leave you with wall space for future purchases. If your collection is constantly changing, consider mounting long metal rods, painted the same color as the walls, at ceiling height. This will enable you to hang pictures from fine cording and then adjust the groupings as you acquire new works and retire others.

OPPOSITE *Slide a tiered console table under a window in a corner of a hallway to hold favorite reading materials. Add a mirror to give the illusion of another window and provide the perfect place for last-minute primping.*

PARTY-READY ENTRIES

Prior to parties, devote some preparation time to the entryway.

- Remove delicate rugs to spare them from the wear and tear of a crowd.

- Plan where guests will put coats, bags, and hostess gifts when they arrive. Clear out the closet well ahead of time; this is not a task to be undertaken right before the first ring of the doorbell.

- If closet space is limited, rent a rolling metal coat rack and shield it from immediate view with a folding screen. A screen is also useful for directing guests away from a busy kitchen or any area of the house that isn't party-ready.

- Greet your guests with a beautiful bouquet, but don't make it so over-the-top that it gets in the way.

- If you are fortunate enough to have a large entry, think of it as an additional living or dining room. For a cocktail party, move in seating and side tables from other rooms, or, for seated dining, rent round tables, long cloths, and small gold-painted chairs.

positive household habits

- Avoid draping guests' coats over a stair rail or hanging them on a doorknob. Use a coat closet, armoire, or other room, or the entryway will quickly take on the appearance of a disheveled dorm room.

- Don't use an entryway closet to store tax files, luggage, or holiday decorations. That sort of storage should be somewhere out of visitors' sight.

- If you have a mail slot, keep a small wicker basket underneath it to keep mail from scattering on the floor.

- Pay attention to scents in hallways, particularly your foyer. Lighting a scented candle can scent an entire hallway. Or store your scented candles in a drawer of a hallway dresser and let the scent waft out from time to time.

Other collectibles that work well in hallway galleries:

- Old maps. These usually look best when framed very simply. A narrow table placed underneath a particularly interesting map can hold a collection of magnifying glasses for examining details.

- Large, framed silk scarves. Hang these on a staircase wall or in an architecturally uninspiring hallway. As with maps, a simple frame style works best. Framing scarves, however, is not a do-it-yourself project. Entrust them to the best framer you know, as the silk must be perfectly taut to look its best.

- Small collectibles like coins, old campaign buttons, or antique pens. Mount them in shadow boxes, which are readily available in camera shops and craft supply stores. Paint the inside of each box a color that offsets the collectibles or line it with fabric.

- Miniature figurines. Add interest to a narrow hallway corner by displaying a collection of small figurines, such as Mexican santos or oriental jade buddhas, on tiny individual shelves. You need critical mass here: two or three will have no decorative impact, even in a small space, but ten, twelve, or more will make a vivid visual statement.

OPPOSITE *Claim a closet from a sliver of hallway space by adding either a wood rod and brackets or a tension-spring pole. Use for anything from rain gear to hiking equipment.*

Showcase Children's Art

Instead of confining children's artwork to the refrigerator door, create a gallery to display it. A hallway is a perfect location. Family and friends can admire the creative outpourings, and you can contain the little masterpieces in one location: The Art Spot. Choose a hallway with plenty of wall space, in a location where the assemblage won't compete with the decor in nearby rooms. A back hall to the kitchen or an upstairs hall between children's bedrooms is ideal. Look for an area where nails won't damage plaster, decorative finishes, or wallpaper.

Use glass clip frames available at art stores and discount drugstores, as well as frame shops. If you're concerned about using glass around young children, opt for the snap-together plastic box frames. Both glass clip and plastic frames come in a variety of sizes. Stock up on a large assortment; budding artists tend to be prolific.

A hall between bedrooms or off a mud room or kitchen also is the perfect place for a family bulletin board. Here family members can post information on upcoming events like soccer games, school plays and pageants, or local festivals and fairs. Make sure the board is generous in size and has a plentiful supply of colorful pushpins.

ABOVE *Create display shelves within a back staircase for meaningful family collectibles from pottery to books, paintings to children's art projects.*

Seasonal Changes

When the Air Is Warm

- Polish brass house numbers and doorknockers so they shine in the sun.

- Update a hall tree. Replace wool coats and parkas with summer-weight jackets and slickers. Hang straw and linen sun hats here, too. Clothing can be a seasonal decorative accessory.

- Deactivate alarms linked to windows and doors usually kept open during warm months. Leave a note by your front door reminding you to shut those doors and windows when you go out.

When the Air Is Cool

- Change the doormat to one that can handle heavy boots and wet weather.

- Keep towels in a hall closet in case a guest, family member, or pet gets caught in a downpour.

- If you don't have a fireplace, use piñon incense from New Mexico. The wonderful fragrance smells like embers of a welcoming fire some- where in the house.

RIGHT *A Victorian terrarium filled with greenery brings a touch of early springtime to a hallway.*

adding life to the living room

Too often the living room is the least used room in the house, an expensive shrine for impressive entertaining, a space rarely entered between parties or major family celebrations. Yet, as its name implies, it should be a room for living. Often it has some of the house's loveliest architectural detailing, as well as some of the best views of the outside. Why let such an attractive space lie dormant awaiting the next onslaught of guests? During private times, it can be used as a reading room, music room, or personal retreat. Set a comfortable chaise lounge near a window for solitary reading and daydreaming. When guests arrive, that same chaise is the perfect spot for two people to sit and have an intimate conversation.

When well organized, the living room can be used on a daily basis and still maintain its party readiness. Most living rooms are decorated with an eye to how they look when people first enter, but what really matters is how the room feels from inside. Organize its decor from the inside out, based on how you want it to work and what furniture arrangements are possible.

The rules of functional decoration are the same whether your home is small or stately. A room for gathering needn't be stiff and formal. Slip-covered hand-me-down furniture and rustic wood benches can be just as effective as custom silk upholstery and highly polished antiques. Let the decoration reflect your own style of living and entertaining. If you are more casual, the room should reflect that. If you enjoy more formal entertaining and think nothing of "dressing for dinner," then a more formal room probably will suit you best. Whatever degree of formality you choose, however, you should rely on functional furniture, effective ways to display artwork and other collections, and some proven party preparation methods to make the room as pleasurable to use as it is to view.

Think of ways to spend more time in this special space. Why not have a friend in for lunch and dine in the living room for a change? Or move your favorite travel books to a special bookcase and use the room for some armchair traveling? Or even start most evenings with a drink there? Living well means using all the spaces in your home.

OPPOSITE *When the weather grows chilly, create a cozy reading corner in the living room. Pull a tea table next to a comfortable chair, make sure there is a good lamp nearby, and bring a soft chenille throw out from its summer storage.*

ABOVE *A backless sofa allows seating access from both sides for parties and serves equally well as a spot for solitary relaxing and reading on a quiet afternoon. A set of three nesting tables stands nearby, and handsome twin cabinets flank the fireplace, providing storage and decorative panache.*

Functional Furniture

Tables. Consider using a tea table instead of a coffee table. Tea tables are higher than traditional coffee tables and make reaching items easy. The additional height may be better for the way you entertain, such as at afternoon teas or group meetings where papers and notepads need to be spread out.

Nested side tables, available in natural wood finishes, richly lacquered colors, or gleaming stainless steel, are living room workhorses. An end table only serves one or two people, while nesting tables can serve many more and then retreat into their neat little nest when not needed.

A long refectory table works perfectly as a library table for piling books and equally well as a dining or buffet table. Adding freestanding bookshelves nearby makes the living room a reading space as well as an entertaining area.

A game table adds a place for a card game, a small dinner, or just a spot to spread out reading material on a weekend afternoon, while a tilt-top table can be tucked into a corner and then opened up when needed.

Desks. A large desk can provide you with a signature look for your living room as well as a spot for letter writing and bill paying. A desk can double as a sofa table and still be a suitable place to draft a quick thank-you note. When set perpendicular to a window, a desk creates a particularly inviting writing spot. The classic Parsons-style table serves equally well as desk, sofa table, or buffet. If used as a sofa table, it can shelter a pair of stools to be pulled out when extra seating is needed.

When entertaining, clear off any writing materials from a desktop and use the surface for a serving area, perhaps with a champagne bucket and a tray of flutes for before dinner or demitasse cups and snifters for coffee and brandy afterwards.

ABOVE *A massive Chinoiserie secretary makes a stunning decorative statement in a formal living room, while providing an appealing place for writing personal correspondence. The numerous drawers offer copious storage capability, and the open cubby holes are perfect display spots for a collection of antique leather-bound books.*

NINE SUGGESTIONS FOR DISPLAYING COLLECTIONS

- Set books with beautiful bindings on an antique ladder with leather-topped steps.

- Gather a group of many small objects onto a large, square glass platter before placing them on a table or shelf.

- Mirror the back of an alcove and add glass shelves to display figurines, sculpture, or pottery.

- Stage small tabletop items atop clear plastic cubes or suede-covered plastic cylinders. Raising them above the table surface will magnify their visual impact.

- Easels bring artworks off the walls and into the room. Use a small easel atop a chest or side table or a large, floor-standing model in a corner of the room.

- Store unframed lithographs in a wooden manger as they do in art stores. You and your guests then can enjoy your entire collection, not just the framed pieces.

- Drape textiles such as Japanese obi, Navaho blankets, or Indian saris over a folding four-panel screen.

- Line a long narrow tray with a collection of candlesticks.

- Fill tall cylindrical glass vases with offbeat collectibles, perhaps matchbooks, champagne corks, or colorful Bakelite bracelets.

A secretary desk with a drop front can be an especially handsome addition as well as a space saver. Just flip the top closed when company is coming to provide more room for people to congregate. A tall secretary with lockable upper glass doors will provide safe display space for valuable collectibles.

Benches, Ottomans, and Stools. Large upholstered benches and ottomans have gained popularity in the design world for their versatility as both seating and handy surfaces. Top with trays or large books to create safe, balanced places for drinks.

If you have a piano, its bench can do double duty. Upholster the top in a rich suede or nubby silk so it provides comfortable extra seating and, from the storage space under the lid, weed out any no-longer-used sheet music to make a place for magazines or books. Be sure to leave enough room around a piano for people to gather. Use a large tray as a spot for guests to set drinks yet keep glasses off the piano's highly polished surface. Or, for more protection, drape the piano top with a decorative cloth or use a dining table pad (cut to size) and covered with a pretty textile.

Bars. If you do not have a built-in wet bar in the living room or a closet that could be converted, you still can create a workable bar area. The classic butler's tray on a stand is a good option and holds a surprisingly large number of bottles and glasses. Another good choice would be a three-tier open cabinet that stands about waist high. Place the most often used bottles, ice bucket, and water pitcher on top, glasses on the second level, back-up bottles on the lowest shelf.

Fireside Seating. A fireplace fender not only makes a strong decorative statement but also provides extra seating. These can be purchased new, but usually bear hefty price tags. Look for one in an antique store or consignment shop, but be sure to have the dimensions of your fireplace with

you when you shop. Until you locate the perfect fender, a simple bench in front of a fireplace can be the best seat in the house on a chilly night.

Inviting Furniture Arrangements

When deciding on furniture placement in the living room, consider not only how the room will look, but also how it will work. One approach is to start with a mixture of upholstered pieces, such as a sofa and two club chairs. Then add easy-to-move side chairs. Complete the seating opportunities

ABOVE *Deeply upholstered seating gathered around a large coffee table creates a living room that welcomes guests. For a large party, the demilune table could serve as a bar and the sofa table as a dessert buffet. The wire-front armoire holds a collection of art books and magazines, accessible for browsing.*

with footstools or an ottoman. Small, upholstered stools can be tucked under a Parsons table or skirted table and brought out when extra seating is required.

Deep sofas should have firm pillows to help provide back support. On a shallower sofa, fewer pillows are required since the sofa back is closer. Don't go overboard with decorative pillows. As pretty as they might be, they shouldn't create a mini-mountain to be moved before a guest can find room to sit down.

But don't deem a sofa a necessity for a well furnished living room. Consider forgoing this large and expensive piece and instead using upholstered chairs, which are far easier to move into different groupings. Armless slipper chairs work well in this capacity. In a small home, where every inch of storage space counts, a built-in window seat with drawers could be a better investment than a freestanding sofa.

Despite your best guess as to where people will congregate, they will create their own sitting areas. Your job is to allow

enough space for chairs and stools to be moved and re-arranged easily. Putting casters on heavy, upholstered armchairs makes them as easy to move as side chairs. Always pair chairs together in groups of two and three. No matter how decorative a single chair looks standing on it's own, it inevitably will draw the shyest party guest to perch like a wallflower at a high school prom. Groups of chairs insure that guests mingle and meet.

Seating is not the only consideration. Be sure to leave areas where groups can stand, otherwise they will all congregate in the hall. And remember to leave plenty of space close to the bar, a spot where people love to cluster.

Entertaining: Being Party Ready

A little pre-party preparation of the living room will ensure an easy, elegant evening. Test drive the room by walking through it as though you were a guest. Think: Where would I put a drink? Is the seating comfortable? Can I navigate the room without fear of knocking over diminutive tables, their surfaces crowded with trinkets? To be party-ready, table surfaces should be left available for glasses and platters of appetizers. Leave spaces. They soon will be filled once the party is underway.

A relaxed guest starts with a relaxed host. If you worry that someone might stumble and single-handedly wipe out your collection of rare porcelain boxes, move the little treasures to

ABOVE LEFT *Placed to allow plenty of room for guests to circulate around them, a pair of side chairs sit party-ready in this inviting living room. For more solitary moments—such as an afternoon of reading—one chair can easily be moved closer to the windows.*

OPPOSITE *Clustering a collection of clay vessels rather than scattering them throughout the living room creates a striking tablescape. The back of the adjacent alcove has been painted a soft lilac color to highlight a collection of vintage mixing bowls.*

a new, temporary location. Then, as every skirt hem rustles by a table leg or jacket sleeve grazes a tabletop, you'll know the worst thing that can happen is a spilled drink. Make sure that doors to a terrace or balcony are easy to navigate, with nothing in the way if groups of people want to wander outside. If you clear the area ahead of time you'll reduce the chance of a favorite ginger jar or pile of vintage hatboxes being knocked over. When preparing your living room for a big party, think bulls in a china shop.

Check the temperature of the room before the guests arrive and again when the party is in full swing. As the room fills, the mercury will rise. Be sure you have a plan for getting some cool air into the room, either through pre-set air conditioning or windows with good cross ventilation.

Flowers and candles add beauty and drama to a party setting; but aim for simplicity over fussiness. Low bowls of flowers are better than over-the-top arrangements. Instead of three or four vases scattered throughout the room, consider massing three dozen roses or a dozen hydrangea heads in a shallow bowl or basket and setting it in a prominent place in the room. The arranging time will be shorter and the impact larger. If you're having a series of events over a week or so, consider using flowering plants instead of fresh floral arrangements. They last longer.

Candlelight gives a glorious glow to evening gatherings, but can create safety issues. Use hurricanes to shield the open flames. While drinking and chatting, people can get perilously close to candles without realizing the danger. This is not the kind of excitement your party needs.

THE WELL APPOINTED BAR

A bar in the living room saves trips to the kitchen or dining room to refill drink or wine glasses during a party. In addition to the wines, liquors, and nonalcoholic beverages you plan to serve, be sure the bar has the following:

- A generously sized ice bucket. A large bowl will work if you don't have a traditional bucket. For a large party, have a filled back-up bucket or bowl.

- Glasses. A wide range, from wine glasses to brandy snifters.

- Wine glass tags. Those decorative little rings that slip into the stem of a wine glass really do solve the mystery of "Whose glass is this?"

- Cocktail napkins. Paper for large parties, cloth for more intimate gatherings.

- Garnishes. Freshly cut lemons and limes, olives, onions, and cherries. Clear glass pitchers of cranberry juice and lime juice if offering cosmopolitans or gimlets.

- A cocktail shaker. Look for an art deco one from the 1920s or '30s in antique shops or a funky one from the '70s and '80s at flea markets.

- Toothpicks. Natural wood ones from China and Japan are particularly attractive.

- A bartender's "cheat sheet"—a guide to mixed drink recipes.

- An absorbent cloth for spills.

For a large gathering, consider hiring a bartender. Mixing drinks is time-consuming and can trap you at the bar for most of the party.

ABOVE *A silver cocktail shaker and flower-filled vase add festive touches to the bar supplies gathered onto a classic butler's tray. Back-up bottles are held neatly in a basket underneath. This set-up is easy to move to whatever spot in the living room works best for a particular gathering.*

Seasonal Changes

When the Air Is Warm

- Place a sisal or sea grass area rug over the existing carpet. Layering these textures helps give your home a seaside look. Stick to natural, undyed area rugs; a dyed rug could bleed color onto a light-colored carpet.

- Change the orientation of the sofa from fireplace to windows or French doors to take advantage of garden views.

- Put away light-sensitive art such as watercolors and photographs during the brighter months. Hang a quilt or baskets on the wall instead.

- Remove skirted tables. The skirts gather dust and need to be fluffed back in shape if they are moved; too much fuss for summer. Replace them with tray tables or hand painted dressers.

- Have a florist prepare a bouquet that will dry well and can be enjoyed all season. Set the arrangement on a table or chest that stands under a mirror to double the floral impact.

- Consider changing lampshades from fabric to paper versions with spring flowers hand painted on them. Or paste postcards from a garden you've visited on a sturdy lampshade.

- Hang a bird feeder by a window. Keep binoculars and a bird identification guide in a nearby table drawer.

When the Air Is Cool

- Shop for a large and handsome firewood holder, perhaps a rough hewn basket, a wicker hamper, or a copper wash cauldron. A generous supply of dry wood is always welcome on chilly days and evenings.

- Light a fire on a weekend afternoon. Fireplaces are not just for the evening. Enjoy the warmth, sound, and smell during gray daylight hours.

- Move a tea table near the fireplace in winter for cozy, informal afternoon entertaining.

- Replace tired silk and linen throw pillows with ones made from richer fabrics: velvets, woven wools, and faux fur.

- Plan for increased indoor entertaining by removing any small, decorative furniture pieces that do little more than consume floor space and restrict party flow. Move them to more private rooms where they can be appreciated.

- Check lamps and lighting. Increase the wattage a bit to counteract the effects of shorter days.

- Move indifferent art works out of the living room. Keep only the pieces there that are most meaningful to you.

PICTURE HANGING POINTERS

Including your favorite artwork in the living room
makes a major contribution to the room's overall
impact. It is also a gift to your guests, allowing them
to enjoy paintings, drawings, or photographs you have
collected. Getting the hang of picture display, however,
can be tricky. Here are some guidelines:

- With a large single picture, avoid the floating-
  in-a-sea-of-blank-wall look by anchoring it visually. Look for a section of wall that offers a
  natural framework: between two windows, in a
  recess, or above a mantle. Or hang it in relation-
  ship with a major piece of furniture, making
  sure the mat and frame styles relate to the furniture's fabric or wood. Placing a picture on the
  wall near a table or chest lets a table lamp provide up lighting.

- Don't hang pictures too high. This is an error
  that designers find over and over when they
  make their initial visits to prospective clients.

- Often the most effective placement for a small
  single picture is extra low. Hang it just inches
  above a tabletop, nestled beneath a taller lamp,
  or alongside the fireplace, aligning the top edge
  of the frame with the top of the mantle.

- A pair of pictures often looks more interesting
  stacked one above the other rather than hanging
  side-by-side. If the two are different sizes, hang
  the smaller underneath the larger. Or instead of
  placing a matching pair right next to each other,
  hang a differently shaped picture in between, perhaps an oval between two squares or rectangles.

- With more than three pictures to group, start
  with the largest as the anchor. Lay it on the floor
  and experiment with placing the others around
  it. Then cut out sheets of brown paper the size of
  the pictures and attach them lightly to the wall
  with masking tape to judge the overall effect of
  the arrangement.

ABOVE *Meticulous picture placement creates an impressive art wall in this spacious living room. Six identically framed works hang in tight formation—centered over the sofa, flanked by vertically hung pairs of larger works, and crowned with a trio of smaller pieces. Nearby, a large drawing is visually anchored by its position above a demilune table, and another trio of large sketches is hung vertically from floor to ceiling. Smaller works propped on the tabletop and leaning against the wall add a touch of informality to an otherwise highly formal arrangement.*

creating a double-duty dining room

The dining room is often the most theatrical room in the house, providing the stage for fine food, good conversation, and celebrations large and small. Organization facilitates all the productions held here, but involves more than china and silverware storage and the care of fine linens. A well-organized dining room has a dual personality: party-ready for guests, yet just as comfortable for daily use.

OPPOSITE *A massive Chinese cabinet serves as a buffet with plenty of storage. Despite the strong decorative elements displayed on the top, plenty of space remains for a tray of drinks or a platter of appetizers. Two large vases stand ready to hold flowers or branches.*

RIGHT *A charming Shaker buffet holds a plethora of linens, silverware, and serving pieces. Wheels on the dining table make it easy to move closer to the fireplace for winter dinners or nearer the windows in warmer months.*

Functional Furniture

Tables. Dining tables come in a wealth of shapes and sizes, from rectangular refectory-style to oval, painted country pieces. Choose a style that suits not only the room's design but also your own entertaining style.

You don't have to fill the room with a massive table if you only give a few large, seated dinners a year. Perhaps the dining room will seem more inviting the rest of the time if you select a smaller table and then make some stylish adaptations when you need more seating space.

A round table that is forty-eight inches (122 cm) in diameter can gain room for more place settings with the addition of a sixty-inch (152 cm) round top. A temporary top requires only the most rudimentary carpentry skills and a minimal investment in materials. Plywood or pressboard are fine. Do, however, have it hinged down the middle so it's easier to carry and store. Table clips will help keep it stable, and a floor-length cloth will make it stylish.

Two matching square tables can be joined to create one large rectangular table when the guest list grows. After the party, keep one table in the dining room and move the other to a corner of the living room for games or to display books. Or move it into an office or a bedroom window alcove. Tables are infinitely useful throughout the house.

Seating. An assortment of chairs is often a better fit for different body types—as well as more visually interesting—than a set of four, six, or eight matching chairs. If a random assortment sounds too eclectic for your taste, consider buying interesting chairs in pairs to maintain a thread of design continuity.

Armless chairs tend to work better in dining rooms where the seating tends to grow crowded. Chairs without arms take up less space and are easier to snuggle right up to

each other. Even a small, curved sofa (for a round table) or a casual daybed (for a rectangular one) can spring into action as extra seating.

If your personal style tends towards larger, deeper seating, make sure the seat depth can be adjusted for a guest by the addition of a small throw pillow. No use making an adult feel like a child in a big chair.

Banquettes make wonderful seating alternatives. There is no law, written or unwritten, that the table has to sit in the dead center of a dining room. An L-shaped banquette set into a corner and used as some of the seating for a table moved nearby will give you a gracious dining area, yet provide more floor space for other furnishings. Use the found space for a large armoire for linens and storage, a floor-to-ceiling bookcase with two comfortable reading chairs placed close by, or even a desk and chair set off by a great-looking screen.

Or pull the table next to a window with a built-in window seat. The advantage of this scheme is that the window seat can have pull-out drawers underneath the cushioned seat, a perfect storage spot for large trays and seasonal linens.

Don't skimp on the cushions for banquettes and window seats. If made from foam, they should be at least three inches (8 cm) thick. For more luxuriously comfortable seating, have cushions made that incorporate springs.

Benches are another good seating option. Long Meeting-House-style benches can be tucked under the table when not in use or moved to a hall or upstairs landing. An upholstered bench that usually sits at the foot of the bed can be borrowed from a bedroom, or one with a woven rush seat, usually housed on the back porch, can be brought into the dining room to provide more seating.

Armoires. Armoires, if fitted with sturdy shelves, can hold an impressive amount of dishes, from stacks of buffet plates to oversized serving platters. If your china collection is not too extensive, there may even be room on one of the shelves for a stereo. Having the majority of your dishes stored in one spot makes table setting both easier and more open to creativity. Pieces you can't readily see seldom make it onto the table, but when you have your grandmother's fish plates or the soup bowls you bought in Paris right in front of you, you think of ways to incorporate them.

ABOVE *During daylight hours this dining area, banked with book-shelves, serves as a library, its spacious table an ideal spot for spreading out books. In the evening, the books can easily be returned to their proper shelves and the table can be set for a seated dinner or a casual buffet.*

ABOVE *Simple built-in cabinetry controls dining room clutter. A silver pitcher, easy to fill with flowers, and a pair of neo-classic candlesticks keep the room attractive and party-ready.*

As a design element, an armoire is particularly useful in a combination living room/dining room or in a loftlike space, where it creates a sense of separation between areas.

Buffets and Cabinets. Buffets offer up a serving space on top with roomy storage below. Interiors can hold your favorite linens as well as china, but this storage space must be organized. Consider tying sets of napkins together with grosgrain ribbon, moving tablecloths to a closet to hang (discouraging wrinkles), and sorting silverware by type and size into drawer dividers lined with Pacific cloth.

Buffet styles vary, from designs with full lower cabinets to ones on high legs that offer less storage but more style. Don't let the open space below a buffet go to waste. Line up three identical wicker hampers underneath for storing linens—or even household files. They will look great, and no one will know the contents. Or keep two upholstered stools tucked below the buffet and pull them into action when you need extra seats. Stacking wooden boxes, whether they are rare Japanese writing boxes, round American Shaker boxes, or even well preserved vintage traveling trunks, add storage capacity and style to a dining room.

China cabinets and hutches are an appealing way to store and display your favorite serving pieces and dishes. Most also have several drawers below the glass-enclosed or open-shelved top portion, which makes storage and organization of linens and cutlery a breeze. But once the china on display is removed and the table is set, the empty shelves look forlorn. Change them from a problem to perfection by filling them with decorative pots of trailing ivy or a bevy of bud vases holding flowers. Keep a focal point a focal point.

If the upper cabinet does not have doors, light a few small votive candles for effect. Another clever way to hide the fact that the china is gone is to buy an assortment of small, post-card-sized mirrors and line them up on each of the shelves to act as an interesting visual distraction. That way, if a few plates or platters are left on the shelf, their number seems to double in the mirrors.

Useful Additions

A Tea or Drinks Cart. Pull a tea or drinks cart next to the head of the table to hold the roast for carving, or have one standing in a corner with dessert plates and coffee cups ready to roll into the living room after the main course.

A Butler's Tray. A butler's tray is another good spot to carve a Thanksgiving turkey, keep extra bottles of wine handy, or hold a cake, ready for cutting.

A Folding Screen. Use a folding screen to keep guests out of the dining room until the "reveal," or to hide the kitchen door and all the frenzy behind it. A screen is also a way to add another decorative focal point to the room. Consider one upholstered in cognac-colored leather, a wooden one wallpapered to match the walls, or one fashioned from three salvaged interior doors hinged together and painted.

Mirrors. Mirrors add light and sparkle while increasing visual space. But it can be very disconcerting to catch a glimpse of yourself in mid-chew. Hang mirrors high enough to reflect light but not faces.

CREATING A MOOD

Setting a festive mood in the dining room requires only a little attention to detail. To make a meal memorable:

- Use your good china for at least one course. If you can't face the thought of hand-washing dozens of plates, use ones that can go in the dishwasher for the first and main courses and then finish the meal with your most exquisite and delicate dessert plates.

- Light candles, even on warm nights. They set a mood you can't get with electric light. But make sure to use unscented candles. Food aromas shouldn't have any competition.

- Always use cloth napkins in the dining room. The luxury and style far outweigh the task of extra laundering.

- If there are more than four people, use place cards. People love knowing where they are supposed to sit. Even if the party was put together at the last-minute and the writing on the cards rushed, place cards make it appear that you have things together.

- Don't overwhelm the room with tributes to floral artistry. The focus of the dining room should be the food and the friends. If you love large floral arrangements, set them on the buffet or sideboard.

Same Room, Other Uses

In many homes, the dining room is a big, beautiful space that might as well have a velvet rope draped across its entrance. Holidays, birthdays, and occasional dinner parties bring it to life, but too many of its days pass with no more activity than a little dusting or vacuuming. Why squander the room's possibilities? Instead, consider outfitting it so it can house other activities without losing its primary purpose of providing a place to share food, family, and friends. In addition to setting up the space as a dining room, consider these part-time uses:

Library. Built-in bookcases, where books share shelf space with serving pieces, candlesticks, and decorative china, create a setting as conducive to literary pursuits as culinary ones. A dining table makes an ideal and generous library table with plenty of space to spread out reading matter. Include a comfortable reading chair and good floor lamp in one corner of the room. As long as the chair's style and upholstery complement the rest of the room's decor, it will not look out of place.

Art Gallery. Whether you blanket the dining room wall with a collection of Japanese woodcuts, as Monet did in his dining room at Giverny, or keep the furniture sleek and minimal to allow room for a collection of contemporary sculpture, you'll discover that it's a joy to dine amongst your treasures. Lighting is important here. Consider bringing in an expert to advise you on how to spotlight your artwork while maintaining an appealing light for dining.

Home Office. Use the dining table as a desk and keep computer equipment and supplies in built-in or freestanding cabinets.

OPPOSITE *Beautifully framed bird prints, hung ceiling high, set the theme for a handsome dining room that doubles as a hobby area. An armchair, side table, and floor lamp grouped off to the side create a comfortable reading spot near the French doors. The enormous firewood basket combines good looks with practicality.*

Music Room. Often the dining room offers good acoustics and a measure of privacy not found in other areas of the house. Many musical instruments are intrinsically beautiful; a piano, harp, or cello would look wonderful in the room, although you might want to consider another location if your preferred instrument is a massive drum set. Designate a cabinet to hold sheet music.

Game Room. As long as the dining table is not too large, it can double as a spot for playing cards or board games. Again, the organizational trick is to designate storage space for the game paraphernalia—perhaps in the space underneath a window seat or in a vintage trunk tucked between the legs of a china cabinet. If the chair upholstery is fragile, have some sturdy canvas slipcovers made to use when the room is in game-playing mode. Whisk the covers off when dinner guests are due.

Organizing for Successful Dinner Parties

Try things out before the party—not just the recipes but also the presentation. Check that the new candles you bought really are dripless, that the new tablecloth looks as good with the wallpaper as you thought it would, or that your large soup bowls really are big enough to hold the osso buco. If you're having a buffet, lay out all the serving pieces and leave a note on each piece as to what food it will contain. When time gets tight, a helper can easily identify what goes where.

Shop for a large, footed creamware bowl or tureen that can become an instant centerpiece with the addition of a mound of fresh fruit. Green apples, oranges, a mix of lemons and limes, or a pile of pomegranates all work well for this.

If you're serving olive oil as well as butter with the bread, keep the oil containers on small trays in case drips form down the sides. This saves your linens or table top from potential damage.

Knowing what works and what doesn't saves time and worry. Make notations in your household journal after a party ends. What vase did the tulips look best in? What color ivy did you use in the cachepots—solid green or variegated? Likewise for silverware. If you noted that no one used the salad forks last time, perhaps you should leave them off the table for this gathering. Record which dishes were tricky to serve, which ones generated requests for second helpings, and what got left on the plates, partially hidden beneath the parsley.

OPPOSITE *Why let a striking room stand empty most of the time? Here, the space is also used as a personal study— an unconventional but highly functional choice. Converting the room back to a dining space requires minimal effort.*

Organizing for Small Get-Togethers

Unless it is a completely catered affair, a large dinner party is a work-intensive undertaking. Enjoy your dining room—and your friends—more often by entertaining on a simpler scale. Here are three suggestions for get-togethers that are easy to organize and don't require elaborate table settings or long hours in the kitchen. After the party ends, be sure to record in your household journal which aspects worked best so you can repeat the event even more easily.

Afternoon Tea: The day before, set the dining room table with your prettiest teacups and small napkins. Polish the silver tea service if you have one, although china teapots look equally charming, and arrange any flowers. Keep flowers and food ultra-simple. A plain pound cake (baked way ahead and frozen) on a rectangular china plate, a cut-glass bowl of fresh strawberries, and two types of tea sandwiches (made early in the morning and stored well-wrapped in the refrigerator) are sufficient fare. If time and energy permit, add a linen-lined basket of warm scones (baked ahead, frozen and re-warmed just before serving).

Soup Party: Use ironstone tureens from the antique collective or deep Fiestaware serving bowls from the thrift store, an eclectic mixture of mugs, and a basket heaped with

French napkins at least twenty inches (51 cm) square. Serve three different kinds of soup—make sure one is vegetarian—and as many varieties of crusty bread as you can round up from local bakeries. Set the soup tureens, mugs, napkins, and breads on the dining room table. No silverware needed, other than the soup ladles. On a side surface, arrange plates of cookies and a large shallow bowl or a wooden dough trough heaped with seasonal fruit that can be eaten out-of-hand.

Dessert Party: Full-meal potlucks can be problematic to organize so that a balanced meal results; dessert buffets are deliberately and delightfully unbalanced. An ample selection of sweets makes this party special, but no one said you had to make them all yourself. As your guests RSVP and ask the inevitable, "Can I bring something," suggest they contribute whatever cake, pie, tart, pudding, or cookies they enjoy making. Even a nonbaker can contribute a bowl of fresh or stewed fruit. Have the table set with footed pressed-glass compotes, jadeite cake stands, majolica platters or whatever serving pieces you collect and enjoy showing off. Stacks of small plates, good-looking paper napkins, and a basket of forks will complete the table setting.

OPPOSITE *Set the table early for a dinner party to guarantee getting every detail right. Being prepared means being relaxed when guests arrive.*

RIGHT *A dessert buffet is set up on a well-worn gate-leg table in this rustic dining room. Footed glass compotes make simple fruit desserts look festive.*

getting control
of the kitchen

For all the sustenance and pleasure food offers, its storage, preparation, and clean-up create constant demands on a kitchen. Whether your own kitchen is a nostalgic nod to vintage decor or a sleek, stainless steel shrine to modern design, its fundamental lifestyle challenges are the same: How do you create maximum storage, corral clutter, and maintain a semblance of order without hiring a full-time staff? Some answers follow.

LEFT *Sturdy chrome-legged stools and a narrow worktable on wheels quickly convert one end of this kitchen into a cheerful eating area. Centered between the windows, an antique wall cabinet holds dishware within easy reach.*

OPPOSITE *A tomato red work table adds a punch of contrasting color to this cozy lime and olive green kitchen. Mounted on casters, the small, tiered table quickly shifts from stove-side work space to informal eating spot for one or two when moved next to the French doors and paired with a stool or two.*

Functional Furniture

As with every other room in the house, carefully chosen functional furniture helps immensely. Setting up spacious and accessible storage for food, cookware, and dishes will smooth out a lot of bumps on the road to organization, but establishing ways to control clutter and maintain cleanliness and order may be the most important aspects of making the journey a pleasant one.

Cabinets, Dressers, and Armoires. Instead of adding more built-in cabinetry to the kitchen in pursuit of surface and storage space, move in a freestanding cabinet, such as the base of an old hutch, a breakfront from a dining room, or a painted dresser. Add a marble or stone top for an easy-to-clean surface. Place the piece at the end of a bank of cabinets to extend counter space, next to the stove for a food prep and pan storage area, or between the cooking and eating areas as a room divider. Convert a small corner to a storage spot by putting an antique pie safe there. One with a wire mesh front will provide visible storage, while a pierced tin front will hide less interesting items.

Walk-in pantries are wonderful, but if you can't sacrifice a closet or give over cabinet space, consider a small·armoire instead. Retrofit the interior to hold your favorite spices, oils, vinegars, and other cooking staples, or make the armoire your baking supplies center. Stock an upper shelf with cooking chocolate, almond paste, and other specialty ingredients and store measuring cups, cupcake pans, tart tins, and baking sheets on the lower levels. Dedicate one shelf to a row of mixing bowls in a range of sizes.

Tables. Central worktables work well as both extra prep areas and casual dining spots. Make sure there is storage space underneath to maximize the potential of an additional piece of furniture. On a shelf under the table, store clear canisters filled with the dried pastas, herbs, grains, and spices you use most often. Not only will you have your

favorite ingredients handy to the work surface, but you also can see when supplies need replenishing. Mount wheels on the table's legs to make it easy to move when needed. Large tables are ideal, but even a relatively small, old, square chopping block can do double duty as a work area and a place for quick breakfasts. Just add a chair or two.

Seating. Keep a counter stool handy in the kitchen. It's a good place to sit while you're chopping vegetables or to lean while stirring a long-simmering risotto. Step stools are invaluable in the kitchen when you need access to upper cabinets or even just to change a light bulb, but utility need not negate style. Look for an antique library ladder or a vintage chrome step stool to do the job.

In a small eating area, use folding metal French garden chairs for extra seating. When not in use, the chairs can hang from sturdy pegs on the wall or be stored in a nearby storage closet or mud room.

OPPOSITE *Steal storage space from a hallway adjacent to the kitchen by outfitting closets with sturdy shelves and glass-front doors. China and glassware are easily accessible, and, when not in use, add color and texture to the passageway.*

ABOVE *A massive, marble-topped baker's table functions as a kitchen island, providing both a work surface and a buffet area for informal entertaining. The sturdy lower shelf adds easy-to-access storage space. A footed white porcelain bowl heaped with green apples and a two-tier plate stand holding grapes and dried apricots are simple but effective decorative touches.*

SIX SIMPLE WEEKEND PROJECTS

Some basic carpentry skills and a day or two of labor can produce terrific storage solutions. And no one ever said the labor has to be yours. If sawing and hammering are not your idea of the way to spend a weekend, hire a handyman to execute any of the following ideas.

- Add a row of four-by-six-inch (10 by 15 cm) cubbies underneath an overhead cabinet. Use the spaces to organize mail, tickets, and other paperwork.

- Hang an open cabinet with shelves near the kitchen dining area. Stock it with your most frequently used dishes to make table setting easy.

- Sliding pallets spaced six inches (15 cm) apart in a cabinet near the kitchen table keep placemats and napkins orderly and accessible.

- A broom closet wastes valuable space if filled only with brooms and mops. Move them to hangars on the back of another door, perhaps in the laundry or mud room, and add shelves to the closet for china storage. A glass-front door will show off colorful dishware. Or commandeer a catchall closet in an adjacent hallway and fit it with shelves and multipane glass doors. You'll find you use more of your dishware collection if it's on display.

- In the eating area, build a simple banquette with deep drawers underneath. Keep family games, linens, and back-up household supplies here. For a simpler variation, omit the drawers and just leave large cubbyholes underneath the seating surface. Outfit these with big baskets with sturdy handles.

- Install an interior Dutch door. Keep the lower half closed when heavy cooking action requires that children and guests stay out. With the top half open, you still can socialize.

OPPOSITE TOP *Open shelves over a kitchen work area keep frequently used dishes and condiments close at hand.*

OPPOSITE BOTTOM *Two rows of cubby holes above a kitchen desk provide organized and easily accessible storage for mail and other family paperwork.*

Cutting the Clutter

The key to cutting kitchen clutter is clear: If you put things away, clutter vanishes. Yet acting on this simple truth can be surprisingly difficult. Putting some systems in place will make the pursuit of a clutter-free kitchen a lot easier, but success depends on persistence as well as planning.

Start by clearing the counters. Some things, of course, should remain out full time: perhaps a coffeepot, a standing mixer, a few canisters, the salt and pepper shakers. Everything else should be evaluated as to how often it's used. If you seldom eat toast, store the toaster in a cabinet. If you only make waffles one Sunday a month, don't let the waffle iron hog valuable counter space. Mount the microwave underneath an upper cabinet or on a shelf supported by decorative metal brackets, which can be found in salvage yards.

If TV-watching is a must in your kitchen, have the set mounted under, or even better, inside, a cabinet. Treat kitchen radios and stereos the same way.

Once you have dispatched the rarely used electric egg poacher, blender, fondue pot, or yogurt maker to a cabinet, closet, basement, or charity resale shop, it's time to deal with the daily influx of mail. One day's mail, tossed on the counter, makes a minor mess. In another day or two the small pile becomes a substantial stack, and in a week, the stack has morphed into a major morass. You must devise a system, one as simple as a basket that you sort through whenever it threatens to overflow or as elaborate as a set of custom-built cubbyholes above a kitchen desk. The only essential is that everyone in the family understands the system and adheres to it.

Dealing with soiled dishes is another continuing commitment. Establish a system of alerting family members if dishes in the dishwasher are clean or dirty. Always end the evening with dishes in the dishwasher or washed and drying near the sink. While it may take some unwelcome effort on busy evenings, remember that you'll be greeted in the morning by a clean kitchen, which gives a good start to the day.

As in other rooms, kitchen storage is simpler to maintain if you have designated containers. Organize cooking utensils like whisks, wooden spoons, and spatulas in ceramic vases, pitchers, or open canisters. Keep like items together, such as whisks in one, spoons in another. Your eye will go right to the utensil and the size you need. Use shallow French wicker baskets to hold fruit and vegetables. Store the baskets on the lower shelves of an island, baker's rack, or open cabinet.

Substantially reducing the clutter is the goal here. Eliminating it completely is unlikely, so camouflage is permitted. For instance, if your upper cabinet doors are glass and you are unable to keep the interiors picture perfect, add a small curtain to the back of each door to conceal the chaos until you can tame it.

OPPOSITE *Quirky white wooden shelves provide sink-side storage and decorative pizzazz. Less frequently used pieces occupy the top level, while easier-to-reach shelves are outfitted with a rack for hanging wine glasses and vertical dividers for holding plates.*

positive household habits

Minor additions to your kitchen routines can reap major long-term benefits. If you only incorporate one of the following suggestions into your permanent behavior, make it the first one.

✣

- Clean as you go while cooking. It only increases pre-meal work time by a few minutes, and knowing the kitchen counters are tidy lets you linger at the table longer at meal's end.

- Place several garbage bags at the bottom of your garbage can. When you remove a filled bag, a new bag will be ready. Consider casters for the garbage can so you can wheel it where you need it. Empty garbage and recycling cans before they get completely full. Cans that teeter on the brink of overflowing will become towering terrors when someone adds a single milk carton or soda can. Each time you leave the house, tote a bag of garbage to the outside cans. This simple ritual will help eliminate unpleasant kitchen smells.

- Install small towel bars and hooks where you need towels the most, around the sink or by a prep area. You should be able to look, reach, wipe, and then return the towel to its holder rather than dropping it in a damp heap on the counter. Keep a small whiskbroom and dustpan for quick counter sweeps of leafy vegetables, flower cuttings, and spice or flour spills that are made worse when cleaned up with a wet sponge.

- Rotate the dishes you use daily. In many households, only the top five or six plates of a large stack are used over and over. Using ones from the bottom ensures that the wear patterns will be even throughout the set.

- When you buy spices or dried herbs, mark the containers with the purchase date. Three-year-old curry powder or powdery ancient oregano will do little to enhance your cooking.

- Take a periodic inventory of your cutlery. Note missing pieces in your household journal. Check knives regularly to see if they need sharpening.

OPPOSITE *Matching baskets convert a ceiling-high stack of small, open shelves into efficient storage nooks. Baskets on the lower shelves hold the most frequently used items, like napkins and candles. Large, deep baskets underneath the wooden worktable hold place mats and tablecloths, ready for use in the nearby eating area.*

Displaying and Using Collections

Kitchen space is too valuable to allot to collectibles that are merely decorative. Apply your collecting zeal to platters that can come off the wall to serve appetizers, rolling pins that will play a part in your holiday baking, or assorted sizes of vintage picnic baskets that can be stacked in the corner as a handsome pyramid, yet still hold recipe binders, seasonal linens, or back issues of food magazines. Here are more ideas for practical displays of kitchen treasures.

■ Stack two or three jadeite cake stands and use as a multi-tier kitchen fruit stand. The soft green color makes a stunning background for various fruits, from autumn's apples to summer's peaches.

■ Choose one or two upper kitchen cabinets and remove the doors. Use the open shelves to display collections of favorite china or glassware. To highlight the collection even more, paint the cabinet interiors a color that showcases the contents, perhaps bright yellow as a backdrop for blue and white spatterware, dove gray for creamware, or brick red for yellow Fiesta dinnerware.

■ Pull collections from cabinets and drawers to hang on the wall. A row of rolling pins, collage of cookie cutters, or grouping of pottery platters adds decorative interest and frees up storage space.

- The top of the refrigerator or an upper cabinet provides useful storage space, but don't let it be a catchall. Plan the baskets, boxes, or whatever you store there. These are good locations for a collection of vases: out of the way, yet always in view, ready to be retrieved to hold a bouquet of flowers brought in from the garden or grocery store.

- In a pantry, large, clear canisters or cookie jars can hold more that just flour, sugar, rice, or pasta. Fill them with a collection of antique cookie cutters, stacks of individual French tart tins, or an assortment of inexpensive bakelite-handled cutlery reserved for picnics.

OPPOSITE *Dish racks, painted a dramatic and unexpected black, showcase a collection of white dishware, while keeping the pieces close at hand for everyday use.*

ABOVE *After a light meal, dishes and cutlery can be washed quickly and left to dry in a sleek steel holder. A versatile wall-hung grid makes a handy place to hang cooking tools.*

EIGHT QUICK AND EASY WAYS TO INCREASE KITCHEN STORAGE

- A single decorative hook for your favorite sauté pan, mounted as close to the cooktop as possible, will save dozens of steps at every mealtime.

- Unless you bake frequently, don't waste counter space with canisters of flour, sugar, and salt. Instead, fill them with things used every day, perhaps cornflakes, coffee, or instant creamer.

- Transferring the contents of partially full boxes of pasta, crackers, cookies, or cereal into small, stackable plastic containers can be a pantry storage salvation.

- Twin trashcans that pull out from underneath the sink allow speedy sorting for recycling.

- Instead of single-depth "egg-crate" dividers in a drawer designed to hold bottles, install stair-stepped dividers, so shorter bottles are easier to reach.

- Hang a five-pocket file next to the kitchen desk area to hold take-out menus and "must-try" recipes.

- Mount a small shelf at eye level to store your most frequently consulted cookbooks. Relegate the rest to less accessible spaces.

- Place a large, antique galvanized-metal tub near the kitchen table to hold newspapers for breakfast-time reading. When the tub is full, it's time to recycle.

Perfecting a Pantry

Converting a kitchen closet, whether it's small and shallow or a spacious walk-in, to a well planned pantry will add immeasurably to the organization of your kitchen.

First, scope out the available space. If it's a fairly large closet, try to keep a three-foot (0.9 m) open space in the middle when adding shelves, even if this means making the side shelves quite narrow. You want to be able to bend over easily to reach the lowest shelves. (Moreover, narrow shelves are best for canned goods, as different items don't get lost in the depths.) Construct shelves from one-inch (3 cm) thick boards, supported every four feet (1.2 m).

Prefer a higher-tech look? Instead of built-in shelves, use the freestanding, chrome-clad Metro shelving found in many restaurant kitchens. Readily available in four- or five-shelf units, usually ranging from fifty-four to sixty-three inches (137 cm to 160 cm) tall, these sturdy pieces are easy to customize to your storage needs, as you can adjust the shelves in one-inch (3 cm) increments. Use trays or large cutting boards to keep small items from slipping through the metal bars. Add a matching rolling cart with butcher-block top for storage space inside the pantry and additional workspace when rolled out into the kitchen.

A pantry floor provides excellent storage space. Place handled baskets there to hold everything from root vegetables and rolls of paper towels to canning jars, funnels, and tongs. Removing several baskets at floor cleaning time is far easier than gathering up dozens of individual items.

Don't neglect good lighting. Pantry shelves benefit from under-shelf lighting just as countertops do from under-cabinet fixtures. And don't limit your choice of ceiling fixture in the pantry to the purely functional. A small wooden or metal chandelier from the flea market can look terrific painted the same color as the pantry walls. Brighten the pantry with yellow walls to contrast with a blue and white kitchen or create an apple red pantry to open onto a sleek black, white, and stainless steel cooking area. When a pantry gives you a little frisson of visual pleasure each time you use it, you're more likely to keep it tidy.

Add an interesting design element by replacing the pantry's solid panel door with a screen door, either new from the home supply store or recycled from a flea market or salvage shop. A double layer of copper screening fitted into the panels looks particularly striking. Screening not only adds a decorative note, but also allows air circulation, which will banish the musty smell pantries can acquire.

In a small kitchen, consider replacing solid door panels with sandblasted glass, which will give an illusion of space without actually revealing unlovely rows of cereal boxes and soft-drink cans. Or cover the entire front of the pantry door with chalkboard. You'll not only create a convenient family message area, you'll also provide a place for resident young artists to draw while you cook.

OPPOSITE *A walk-in closet blessed with a window houses a cheery pantry. Basket hooks alongside the window and a pot rack above it take maximum advantage of the available space*

ABOVE *Big comfortable seating calls for a generously sized coffee table. This one provides a lower shelf for storing books and magazines and has a drawer ideally located to hold remote controls. Plenty of top surface space means the table can serve as a display area, informal dining spot, homework headquarters, game table, or footrest.*

organizing the family area

Of all the rooms in the home, the family room most reflects the lifestyles of its occupants. Whether to watch television, listen to music, or just to gather, everyone gravitates here. As an area for long homework sessions and even longer board game tournaments, children's birthday parties, and informal holiday gatherings, it's a room that should work as well for one person quietly reading a book as it does for a dozen people shouting over the Super Bowl.

Along with all the activity that takes place in the family room comes a host of storage and clutter-control issues. If these are ignored, a room with so much potential quickly becomes burdened by a morass of newspapers and magazines, backpacks, briefcases, DVDs, and board games. Bookshelves become jumbled catchalls, and no one can find the remote control.

Random "straightening up" isn't the solution. Instead, look at your family's daily habits for keys to organizing the family room. For example, if a child's backpack and homework assignments always end up on or near the coffee table, perhaps it's time to stop hoping he'll use the desk in his bedroom and just be grateful the work is getting done. To eliminate tripping over the backpack or worrying about school papers getting mixed in with magazines and mail, create a specific storage solution. Place a large basket under the coffee table or some cubby cubes in a bookshelf, for instance, and reserve these spaces for school papers and books.

Do family members clutter a tabletop or bookshelf with laptop computers, personal organizers, and cell phones plugged in for recharging? Perhaps the table or shelf is near the only handy electrical outlet. Consider having an outlet installed inside a cabinet so this equipment and its unsightly cords can be hidden while their batteries recharge.

Seemingly minor furnishing and decorating decisions can have major impacts on subsequent storage. Choosing the best coffee table for your family's needs, adding a well outfitted desk, and getting overstuffed bookshelves under control will benefit everyone. Children, and many adults, tend to dump, stack, and abandon their personal belongings on the easiest-to-access surface—including the floor. Throughout the home, clutter accumulates when there is no logical, easy-to-use place to store things. The family room's heavy traffic makes it particularly susceptible, but once you start looking at how it needs to function for your family, you will soon see ways to make it more organized. This chapter is packed with ideas and inspiration to help.

Don't be unrealistic about organizational goals. Establish appropriate and easily accessible storage, devise a few basic rituals about returning items to these storage spots, and don't confuse organization with perfection. Leave the perfect families to 1950s television shows. They were boring then and would be boring now.

Copious Coffee Tables

A family room coffee table needs to be far more than a place to set down a drink or toss a half-read magazine. The right piece can offer some of the room's most accessible storage, which makes finding a table that is hardworking as well as good-looking worth considerable effort. Whether you are shopping for a new piece or want to improve a table you already own, you have a multitude of choices. Skip iron and glass tables, however. They do little for storage and require too much maintenance in a family living area.

Coffee tables didn't become a part of our decorative ancestry until well into the last century. Before that, higher tea tables were more prevalent, but as Americans began to slouch and lounge, they needed lower tables for coffee, tea, and other beverages. Remember two basic guidelines when selecting a coffee table: get the height right for the adjacent seating and select a table as large as your space allows. With coffee tables, the larger the better.

Trunks make terrific storage-rich coffee tables. Consider a lacquered Chinese or Japanese trunk, an old military footlocker, a big wicker hamper, or an antique leather car trunk. If your search for trunks comes up empty, perhaps you could move your grandmother's cedar chest from the guest room to the family room and put it to work as a coffee table.

Trunks often have irregular tops, dented from years of travel. Create a level surface and protect the fragile top of a vintage trunk or chest by pairing it with a large tray. Keep in mind that trays don't have to be rectangular. Square, round, and oval shapes all look good on rectangular trunks or tabletops and give the surface a sense of visual organization. Depending on the decor of your room, a Victorian tole-painted tea tray, a heavily woven raffia tray, or even a primitive Mexican dough trough can organize the top of your coffee table and look great while doing it.

Old pine flat files, once used to store maps or architectural drawings, make fabulous coffee tables: their five or six slim drawers are perfect for storing everything from DVDs to board games. If the look of your room is more high tech, use a contemporary version of an artist's flat file, available in either wood or metal. A pair of square, lidded storage cubes could substitute for a coffee table, but four cubes gathered together would provide more storage and a stronger design statement.

As you wander through flea markets and antique shops, consider the unusual. Even a weathered Maine lobster trap could become a table with the addition of a wood or glass top. The space between the weather-beaten bars provides storage. If you're fortunate enough to find an old farm table with drawers, don't be afraid to cut down the legs so it's the right height. Take what you find interesting and appropriate and make it work for your particular space and lifestyle.

ABOVE *A slatted shelf creates space to keep favorite reading matter handy, and it frees the tabletop for a dramatic arrangement of cherry blossoms. Instead of books and magazines, the shelf could hold a folded cashmere blanket.*

OPPOSITE *Nestled on the lower shelf of a coffee table, a pair of deep baskets provides storage for newspapers, magazines, board games, or even homework assignments. The baskets are easy to tote to other parts of the room and easy to return to their coffee-table home.*

A REFUGE FOR REMOTES

Whether you operate your media equipment via multiple remote controls or a single, elaborately programmed model, you need to establish a specific storage spot for these unattractive pieces of hardware. But just because the control units themselves are aesthetically lacking doesn't mean their containers need to be. Ignore the boring mini-grandstand versions usually suggested in favor of a container that's both handsome and unexpected. Some of the following suggestions might already be in your home; others are easy to locate in import stores, antique shops, or flea markets. After you turn off the television or shut down the stereo, return the remote to one of the following:

- An old leather jewelry box,

- The overturned lid of a covered basket (use the basket base to store program guides),

- A bright red Lucite box,

- An oblong wooden Chinese rice container,

- A round ultra-simple Shaker wooden box,

- A vintage 1930s sewing basket,

- A box fashioned from faux books,

- An English tea caddy,

- A fabric-covered stationery box.

Functional Furniture

Side Tables. Whether you call them side tables, occasional tables, or lamp tables, these handy small pieces of furniture offer big opportunities for adding storage space without spending much cash. Each table you incorporate is an opportunity to provide a pocket of organization. Why place a top-and-legs-only table next to a chair when you can find similar-sized pieces with a drawer or two?

Look around your house. An old nightstand, long since relegated to the attic, may need little more than a fresh coat of paint to update it for family room use. Flea markets and consignment stores are treasure troves of reasonably priced small tables. Some may need refinishing; others may need entire new tops. But the amount of new wood—or even marble—needed to top a vintage two-drawer oak file cabinet, a funky hexagonal drum table from the 1930s, or a narrow telephone table from the 1950s is so small that the finished piece should still qualify as a bargain.

Desks. A desk for nearly every room is a mantra for the organized home. Here in the family room, outfit a desk so each family member can use it effectively. Be sure it includes at least two deep drawers: one to hold files and another to hold phone books suspended from slim metal rods. In a top drawer, keep a laminated list of frequently needed and emergency phone numbers, as well as a list of family and friends' birthdays and anniversaries. Atop the desk, a lidded basket of birthday and anniversary cards—which you refill regularly—plus a box filled with stamps, will encourage children and adults alike to remember important occasions.

Game Tables. Game tables are too often overlooked in the search for functional furniture. Once an essential part of any family gathering area, they deserve a return to popularity. Not only do they provide a place for board games, card games, and mammoth jigsaw puzzles, they also serve as handy spots to do homework or plunk down a laptop computer. Covered with a floor-length tablecloth, a game table works well as a second food station or bar table for parties. If floor space is limited, look for smaller-scale game tables designed primarily for chess, checkers, or backgammon. Often these handsome pieces have a game board painted on one side of a reversible wooden top, with storage underneath.

Sofa Tables. Sofa tables nestle up to the back of a sofa and provide a place to set lamps, books, and baskets within easy reach. Beneath their functional top surface, however, lie a bevy of storage opportunities. Even a single lower shelf can hold large baskets; multiple shelves or enclosed cabinet areas can store everything from photo albums to extra supplies for the desk.

If books are overflowing from other bookshelves, place a low bookcase behind the sofa. Or consider creating a sofa table

from a pair of stepped end tables, placed side-by-side. Ones with three steps each are ideal, with the lower steps providing easy-to-reach spots to store magazines, games, and puzzles. Before shopping for any of these useful pieces, double-check your sofa measurements: a sofa table always should be slightly lower than the sofa back.

ABOVE *A cheery red desk invites family members to write a thank-you note, pay bills, or complete a homework project. Deep drawers provide space for files, maps, and manuals. Nearby bookshelves keep reference materials handy.*

OPPOSITE *Add additional shelves to a primitive painted cupboard to create display space for favorite collectibles. Store less visually appealing items, such as board games or old magazines, in the closed cabinets below.*

The Case for Organized Bookshelves

In the homes of book aficionados, family room bookshelves quickly reach their maximum capacity. To maintain order, it's important to schedule regular weeding sessions to cull out unwanted books and dispatch them to the local library or charity resale shop. Books you seldom glance at but still hesitate to discard should go into well labeled boxes in a storage area. Always note the specific titles and storage location in your household journal so you can locate a book quickly—even years later.

To make specific books easier to find, group them by category and then separate each category, using decorative elements as bookends. An earthenware crock filled with magnifying glasses, a collection of vintage reading glasses mounted in a shadowbox, or a small painting or favorite photograph on an easel can all serve to keep your books separate but still aesthetically pleasing. Reserve one portion of a shelf for reference books. Having a dictionary, the-saurus, and atlas handy means everyone in the family is more likely to consult them.

If you regularly loan books to friends, establish a record-keeping system. Whether you list book titles and borrowers' names in a small notebook or on index cards stored in a decorative box, keep it on a designated bookshelf.

Customize storage for magazines by placing a small wine rack on a bookshelf. Just roll the magazines and slip them into the bottle slots. Or borrow an idea from European cafés: lean a slim decorative ladder against the wall and drape the magazines over the rungs. For complete sets of magazines you want to save, consider having them bound. Leather bindings make a particularly handsome decorative state-ment, while more budget-friendly cloth bindings come in a wide range of colors.

Many built-in bookcases combine open shelves in the upper portion with enclosed storage in the lower, but if you remove some of the lower cabinet doors and shelves, you can cre-ate alcoves for large rectangular baskets. Use these to hold magazine and newspapers neatly. To control the chaos that

back issues can cause, establish a firm habit: when a basket is full, send several inches of reading matter from the bottom of the pile to the recycling bin.

Finally, a built-in bookcase next to a fireplace can provide handsome, as well as handy, storage for logs and kindling. Line one section with heavy-gauge copper. Be sure it is well lacquered to withstand the moisture that even well aged firewood will release.

ABOVE *A small open cabinet holding wicker trays and baskets stands next to the family desk to supplement storage space for papers and supplies. The sliding library ladder affords easy access to high bookshelves that make maximum use of available wall space.*

ORGANIZING WITH TANSU

Tansu—which translates loosely as chest or box—is a collective term for a range of freestanding antique Japanese cabinetry that works beautifully in twenty-first-century homes. Most styles feature multiple doors and drawers, making them ideal storage pieces. Whether you invest in a true antique or a more modern copy, the simple yet sophisticated design of a tansu blends seamlessly into contemporary or traditional decor.

- Tansu tops are sometimes unfinished. If you do not plan on stacking them nearly ceiling-high, disguise the exposed tops with slabs of stone, pieces of finished wood, or antique Japanese textiles.

- Tansu make useful end tables. Elevate them on simple metal or wood stands, if necessary, to achieve perfect sofa-side height.

- Pull the sofa well away from the wall and place two tansu at its back to provide far more storage space than found with a traditional sofa table.

- Store CDs and DVDs in the handsome tansulike boxes originally designed as sewing boxes, medicine chests, or calligraphy boxes.

- Place two or more large tansu of similar size side-by-side to create a wall of storage. For additional decorative zing, stack small tansu on top of larger ones.

- For a major infusion of both drama and storage space, flank a doorway with a pair of seven-foot-high (2.1 m) tansu: the stepped cabinets designed to serve as both stair and storage units. Even a single-stepped tansu provides a wealth of storage space within its drawers and creates abundant shelf space for books, pottery, or flowering plants.

- If your family room sometimes doubles as a guest room, store blankets and pillows in a large futon tansu, a deep cabinet originally designed to hold Japanese bedding.

To learn more and find shopping information on tansu, see the Buyer's Guide section in the back of this book.

OPPOSITE *The multiple doors and drawers of an elegant tansu can conceal organized storage for everything from cassettes and DVDs to supplies for scrapbooking and other crafts.*

positive household habits

Once you have logical (and great-looking) storage systems in place, the three-minute sweep can be an amazingly effective tool for corralling family room clutter. Remember, the goal here is to do this within three minutes. Start stretching it out and soon it will seem more like a burdensome chore than an easy blitz. We suggest this as an end-of-the-evening pickup, but it also works as an effective triage tactic when unexpected company pulls into the driveway.

OPPOSITE *A living space filled with natural light affords storgae solutions that allow multipurpose opportunities for personal and professional use.*

✤

- Gather up newspapers and magazines. Stash already-read sections into the recycling container and sections to be saved in the appropriate storage spots.

- Return books to shelves, videos and DVDs back to their cases, and remote control units to their basket, box, or bin.

- Scoop any abandoned sweaters, socks, or other clothing items into a basket. If feeling merciful, take the basket to the laundry room, where the owners can reclaim them. If feeling annoyed by having picked up the same dirty sweatshirt or gym shoes too many times, hide the basket and make the guilty parties beg.

- Fold blankets or throws neatly and plump up squashed chair and sofa cushions.

- Tote any used dishes or glasses to the kitchen sink.

✤

The three-minute sweep is a major weapon in the never-ending battle against miscellaneous and messy drifts of family-room detritus. One day's accumulation almost always can be dealt with in three minutes. Allow piles to grow for a few days, and you're apt to need a half-hour or more to restore the room to a semblance of order.

Seasonal Changes

When the Air Is Warm

- Put away wool blankets and replace with light-weight cotton or chenille throws.

- If you have the budget or are handy with a sewing machine, consider slipcovers for uphol-stered furniture. Freshen the room with garden-print chintzes, bright awning stripes, or color-washed linen in tangerine, khaki, or lily-pad green. For the purist, white cotton slip-covers turn upholstered pieces into an unobtrusive background for antiques, art, and decorative collections.

- Roll up area rugs and store until cooler weather returns. Let the bare wood shine over the sum-mer months.

- Remove heavy window treatments. In the winter they help to insulate; in the summer they hold the heat.

- Clear out dusty dried-flower arrangements. Replace with fresh flowers and pots of trailing ivy.

- Stock up on plain white pitchers and small color-ful glass vases to showcase informal summer bouquets.

- Fill an unused fireplace with ferns or flowering plants, but be sure to rotate them outdoors regu-larly to keep them healthy.

When the Air Is Cool

- Have fireplaces checked prior to using them on the first cold night. Make sure you have enough dry logs and kindling on hand as well.

- Bring wool blankets and throws out from sum-mer storage.

- Change candles from spring and summer colors like peach, melon, and sky blue to more autum-nal hues like heather, brick, and sage. Note in your household journal the brands you like and which kinds burn the longest. Also note any scents you've found particularly appealing.

- Shorter days mean less light. Move sun-sensitive plants closer to windows. Consider using grow lights in some lamps.

- Vacuum curtains and upholstery. "Spring clean-ing" also applies to cooler months.

- Turn sofa and upholstered chair cushions. Since many fabrics fade when exposed to light, it's best to rotate cushions so fading is even on both sides.

- Store the smaller vases suitable for summer's flower bouquets and bring out larger containers that can hold branches of persimmon, autumn leaves, or pyracantha berries.

OPPOSITE *Invite summer indoors by taking up rugs and dressing upholstered furniture in slipcovers the color of lemon-lime sherbet. Exchange wooden side tables for wicker pieces and keep reading material handy in a basket.*

creating calm
in the bedroom

Bedrooms serve as far more than sleeping spaces. They are dressing areas, reading retreats, and places for family talks on lazy Sunday mornings. Even work sometimes ends up here, which necessitates a place for a laptop, or, better yet, a mini-office tucked into an alcove or converted closet.

Sleeping comfort usually gets top priority when furnishing the bedroom. Too often, however, tremendous time and attention is devoted to mattress comfort and the thread count of sheets at the expense of other important aspects: a copious nightstand top, a reading lamp with clear, bright light, and a comfortable sofa or chair for a contemplative moment alone. Yet these ingredients—along with efficient storage—all contribute to the sum total of an organized and pleasurable bedroom.

Clutter and disarray—from piles of clothing to stacks of half-read magazines—draw your attention, inhibiting relaxation. A room free from clutter actually can improve your sleep, so start with a beautifully dressed bed, and then surround it with furniture that facilitates order and tranquility.

OPPOSITE *A Chinese cabinet—an unexpected nightstand choice—makes a strong decorative statement without overwhelming other furniture pieces. The roomy interior offers plenty of storage space, while the color provides a bright accent.*

Functional Furniture Near the Bed

Significant storage opportunities exist alongside, under, and at the foot of the bed. Take advantage of all three areas.

Beside the Bed. Don't limit nightstands to matched sets, like bookends. Everyone has different requirements for bedside storage; nightstands should be as individual as the people who use them. Nightstand tops get filled—and fast—so think about what you need most by your bed: the latest novel, fresh flowers, and a decanter of water? Or a clear space to set a memo pad and cell phone? Perhaps you want to reserve room for a favorite family photograph or a small painting on an antique easel? Give yourself the gift of adequate bedside space. Dainty tables may provide a graceful look, but they offer little in the way of suitable surface and storage.

A nightstand could be a vintage cast-off, a wicker tray table, or a skirted table with hidden storage for the DVDs you enjoy watching late at night or the back issues of magazines you like to peruse. Even a small library table, with a leather top, can serve as a nightstand. A discarded metal garden table, cleaned and painted with a pretty pastel color enamel, makes an attractive bedside piece. Pair it with a lidded picnic basket to make use of the floor space below.

A dresser makes an excellent nightstand. Its ample top will hold considerable bedside paraphernalia, while the drawers provide clothing storage, or, for the avid reader, hold an array of books. Store paperbacks with the spines up, so specific titles are easy to locate.

Consider using a long coffee table alongside your bed to provide plenty of bedside space. (Style icon Diana Vreeland used this trick.) Or place a sofa table behind the bed. All that surface: Glorious! Whatever style, size, or shape of nightstand you choose, always consider the surface and storage space.

Other nightstand niceties:

- A decorative tray can hold your alarm clock, notepad (for middle-of-the-night inspirations or "to-do" lists), telephone, and bottled water. Grouping necessities on a tray goes a long way toward controlling nightstand chaos.

- If the nightstand has drawers, the top one should be for items you need most: reading glasses, medicine, and the like. Look for pieces with deep, roomy drawers.

- Leave room for a lamp. To free up surface space, you can forego a table-top fixture and use a floor lamp or a wall lamp mounted on a swing-arm.

- No matter how you allot the space atop your nightstand, save a spot for a small vase of flowers.

At the Foot of the Bed. Here is where any bedroom can gain storage space by acquiring a piece of functional furniture. If the room needs more seating as well, consider one of these for the foot of the bed:

- An upholstered bench, with baskets or stacks of books underneath,

- An ottoman with hinged top and storage inside,

ABOVE *Storage opportunities surround the bed. A nightstand with a slim drawer and open interior alongside, a lined wicker basket on casters below, and a dual-purpose bench at the foot all contribute to a well-ordered room.*

OPPOSITE *Carefully selected furniture sets the scene for a serene bedroom. A conveniently placed chair, generously proportioned nightstand, and narrow table at the foot of the bed enhance the room's usefulness. Crisp linens and plump, oversized pillows, perfect for reading in bed, add to the room's luxurious feel.*

- A small sofa with a wicker tray to hold magazines on one of the cushions,

- A curved-ends settee with fabric-covered storage boxes underneath.

For storage without seating:

- A low chest of drawers,

- A stack of vintage luggage,

- A Chinese altar table,

- A rectangular wicker hamper.

Under the Bed. Underneath your bed there is a perfect hiding place for usable storage. If this conjures up memories of mad scramblings to clean up your childhood room, when the space under the bed proved to be the most convenient place to stash a myriad of possessions, this adolescent view of housekeeping isn't far from wrong. It still is an effective storage location as long as it is organized. What's crucial is deciding how to contain the items.

- Use large, square, shallow baskets to store folded blankets and linens. This saves precious closet and cabinet space.

- Lined baskets on rollers can keep a wealth of books and magazines handy for bedtime reading.

- Buy clear, lidded storage bins to hold anything from personal keepsakes to seasonal clothing. A notation in your household journal will keep track of what has been stored where.

- Is there space for collapsible exercise equipment? Could your free weights or yoga mat and block be kept under the bed? It's easy to roll out a few hand weights and start your work out.

- Store collections of flat artwork or paper collectibles like maps, botanical prints, or antique photographs under the bed. Archival museum cases are ideal, but, at a minimum, wrap works in acid-free paper or matting to protect them from chemical damage.

- Keep a collection of 1940s and 1950s luggage pieces filled with clippings, travel photos, and family mementos under the bed. Pull out the suitcases on occasion to take a trip down memory lane.

Other Bedroom Pieces

Once you have established sufficient storage around the bed, it's time to address other areas of the room. Armoires, desks, dressing tables, and folding screens are additional types of functional furniture for organizing a bedroom.

Armoires. Whether a fine antique or a junkshop discovery, an armoire or wardrobe cabinet can work storage miracles. They come in all sorts of sizes and styles from art deco–inspired designs to more primitive-looking pine versions. Local antique marts, collectives, and vintage furniture retailers usually stock a proliferation—from simple one-door cabinets that fit in tiny spaces to two- and three-door designs that require ample wall space yet reward you with abundant storage. Clever labeling of interior drawers, shelves, and racks still survives in some old armoires, making sorting clothing fun, as if you are, for a moment, a part of the past.

While the armoire's original main purpose, providing storage space for clothing, still applies, these roomy cabinets have a multitude of other organizational uses in the bedroom:

- Interiors can be kited out with a small desktop surface and a pullout keyboard tray to create a hidden workstation. Other equipment, like a fax machine (turn off the ringer) or small copier can be placed here. Add a bulletin board or upholstered memo board for visual inspirations and reminders.

- A metal or wood rack can be added to house your expanding shoe collection.

- Stash extra pillows and blankets out of sight but within easy reach.

- Use an armoire as a place to set decorative pillows, throws, and other bed dressing that is removed each night—a much better option than piling it on the floor or burying your favorite chair.

- Set an armoire in a large walk-in closet. You may be reluctant to remove hanging rods to make room for the cabinet, but by adding an

ABOVE *A grand-scale room divider makes a strong contemporary design statement while concealing storage cabinets and a dressing area. Swing lights mounted to the dividing wall save night table space.*

HIDE AND DIVIDE WITH SCREENS

Few decorative accessories work as hard as the freestanding screen. Besides supplying a decorative focal point, screens can camouflage an awkward architectural element, shade a window, or create a cozy corner of privacy within a shared bedroom.

Use a screen to hide anything from a television or unsightly radiators to a rolling clothes rack. Or call on a screen to create a separate space for work or dressing.

If your bedroom does not have an obvious area to screen—an alcove or arm of an L-shaped room would be ideal—consider using a screen as a headboard for a bed floated away from a wall. Leave an eight-foot (2.4 m) space behind the screen for the dressing or work area. Even less space can be useful for storage if outfitted with chests of drawers.

ABOVE *A four-panel upholstered screen makes a pretty headboard while hiding a storage area. Deep baskets can be nested when not in use.*

A screen can consist of well weathered wooden panels or ones elegantly clad with antique leather. Rejuvenate a battered screen by upholstering, slipcovering, or spraying it with automobile paint for a sleek, contemporary look. Wallpaper or découpage are other screen-refreshing coverings.

More screen strategies:

- Most screen panels are basically rectangular in shape, although panel tops can be curved, angled, or even stair-stepped. For bedroom use, look for one that works well with the shape of the headboard, window cornices, or other major architectural elements of the room.

- Rejuvenate an old solid-panel screen by replacing the panels with fabric: anything from crisp, casual canvas to elegant metallic silk.

- Screens with fabric panels within wooden frames are easy to incorporate into a variety of decors. The fabric can be stretched taut, padded, or shirred. Changing one fabric for another is relatively simple. Another plus: because they are lighter weight than most solid-panel screens, they are easier to move from place to place.

- Create your own screen by hinging together three or four tall wooden shutters. Small, hollow-paneled wooden doors also will work. If you can find vintage Chinese wooden doors, you can assemble a stunning screen. The pierced upper sections of the doors allow light to pass through, while the solid lower portions block any unattractive views.

- Curtains can serve as effective and attractive screens; just mount the curtain hardware on the ceiling.

upholstered chair or tufted ottoman, you will have created a dressing room.

- In a large bedroom, line up three armoires of different but complementary designs to provide a wall of stylish storage.

Desks. A desk in the bedroom? Yes. A desk doesn't necessarily signify work. A bedroom desk may be the only quiet place to write thank-you notes, make entries in your journal, or draw up a lengthy "to-do" list.

Unless your bedroom also serves as a home office, you don't need a large desk or one that looks as if it belongs at a corporate headquarters rather than in your private retreat. Think more along the lines of a writing desk: enough room for paper and pen, a compact laptop computer, a lamp, and a few favorite pictures of friends and family. In a small bedroom, the desk can double as a nightstand.

Consider how the desk will enhance the room's style as well as its function. A white wicker desk will impart a fresh, casual look. A narrow gateleg table, in a rustic finish, is another possibility; its folding leaves can provide extra surface space when needed. The simple lines of a Parsons table, finished with a bright color lacquer, would add a contemporary note.

Dressing Tables. Skirted dressing tables not only look attractive but also provide hidden storage. Look for a vintage kidney-shaped vanity from the 1930s or '40s at consignment stores, or create the perfect-size dressing table for your available space by draping an inexpensive table with fabric. A large, rectangular table, its legs cut down, will hide sizable boxes holding out-of-season clothes. Old knee-hole desks also make good dressing tables. Give one a decorative paint finish, rather than a skirt, to preserve access to the side drawers.

If you can find an old three-sided standing mirror—once the standard accompaniment to a dressing table—it will give the

ABOVE *A skirted dressing table adds a touch of romance as well as hidden storage space to a traditional bedroom. A grouping of plates hung on a nearby wall brings an attractive collection out from storage to add visual interest to the room.*

Vintage steamer trunks supply bountiful storage while adding a nostalgic twist to a guest room's decor.

table a terrific look. Other options: a freestanding vintage bureau mirror, an oval standing picture frame filled with a mirror, or a round mirror hung on the wall above.

Create a dressing nook in an alcove or even in a corner of the bedroom. Use a folding screen to define the area and furnish it with a dressing table, mirror, and a chair or stool. Add an old-fashioned hat rack or some sturdy wall hooks for organizing outfits ahead of time. A mirrored screen would be sensational here.

Gracious Guest Rooms

Once a guest room is organized, it will need only a last-minute addition of a small vase of fresh flowers, a few copies of the latest magazines, and a tiny dish of first-rate chocolates to be ready to receive visitors. To reach that point, check that you've done the following:

- Make a place for luggage. A painted wooden bench or antique trunk at the foot of the bed works well. If the room is small, a folding luggage rack can fit into a sliver of space. Flea markets and estate sales often yield folding racks at bargain prices. Replacing worn straps is a simple matter of basting or even gluing decorative fabric around strips of canvas and then stapling the new straps to the frame.

- Empty the bureau drawers. In a home with limited storage, it's very tempting to fill the drawers of a guest room bureau with out-of-season clothing, old scrapbooks, photos awaiting sorting, and other miscellany, but this forces guests to live out of their luggage. If you absolutely cannot keep these drawers empty, at least keep items in baskets or fabric-covered boxes which can be moved quickly and easily to a temporary home just before visitors arrive.

- Provide reading materials. A small, seven-drawer lingerie chest works well in a space-limited guest room. Use some of the lower drawers to hold magazines and books guests might enjoy reading, but update the reading matter regularly. The choices shouldn't remind your guests of being in a doctor's waiting room.

- Offer pillow choices. Stock the guest room closet with both soft and firm options, as well as with an extra blanket. Splurge on a variety of good-looking, sturdy hangers, including some fat, satin-covered ones for fancy blouses and dresses. Wire hangers from the dry cleaners? Not acceptable.

THE ORGANIZED CLOTHES CLOSET: AN UNORTHODOX APPROACH

If repeated attempts to get your main clothing closet under control have failed, it may be time for a more radical approach. Renting a rolling rack for a day facilitates this process but isn't essential.

- Empty the closet.

- Vacuum thoroughly and wipe down any shelves.

- Sort your clothing into types: jackets, slacks, shirt, shoes, and so forth. If you didn't get a hanging rack, pile them on a bench or the bed.

- Visually allocate a section of closet space for each clothing type. This doesn't have to be exact, but you don't want to find you've put back so many jackets and slacks, for instance, that you have no room for skirts, or that you've filled the shelves with handbags and left no space for sweater boxes.

- Now, pick one category and start returning items to the closet, beginning with your favorite pieces. Once you have filled the allocated section, you must stop. No playing the "just-one-more" game.

- Proceed to putting back the next category of garments. Again, move from "favorite" to "less-loved." Stop when the section is filled— filled, not stuffed.

Once the best of each category is back in the closet, it's time to examine the remaining items. Give them to a friend, donate them to a charity resale shop, or pack them away for storage elsewhere. Note in your household journal the location and contents of any stored cartons. Keeping your main closet filled with your favorite pieces will make keeping your wardrobe organized an easier and pleasanter task.

■ Supply a workspace. Even a small writing table
makes a big addition to a guest room. Guests
often feel hesitant to set up a laptop computer,
work on business papers, or even write a letter at
the desk in a family room or home office. Providing
them their own private workspace doesn't require
a massive desk with deep drawers. A small table
with a shallow drawer or two can hold stationery,
pens, stamps, some local postcards, and maps of
the area. Adding a small freestanding mirror to the
desk enables it to double as a dressing table.

ABOVE *Even a small alcove*
can be converted to a cozy
spot for guests. The raised
sleeping surface leaves room
for storage space below.

Seasonal Changes

When the Air Is Warm

- Slipcover a wooden headboard with a perky print or traditional blue-and-white striped ticking. This simple change will give your bedroom an immediate seasonal lift.

- Put heavy oriental rugs away and use rag or braided rugs for the duration of summer.

- Replace bed linens and bed skirts with solid-color pastels and crisp checks. Lighten the colors and lighten the mood. While the bed is stripped, flip and rotate the mattress.

- Exchange down comforters for lightweight cotton blankets.

- Have winter blankets professionally cleaned, then store them in a closet with lavender sachets until autumn arrives.

- Move winter clothing and shoes to the back of the closet or into another storage space. Replace with your summer wardrobe.

When the Air Is Cool

- Retiring to bed early with a good book is a cozy way to combat chilly winter evenings. Buy extra-large pillows to prop yourself up in bed for these reading sessions.

- Increase the wattage in bedside lamps to make reading easier.

- Sort through your bedside reading stash. Discard out-of-date magazines and books you started but didn't find interesting enough to finish.

- Pile quilts or blankets on a trunk or bench at the foot of the bed. Having a warm covering within easy reach is heavenly on a cold night.

- Check electric blankets for frayed ends or wires before using for the first time.

- Keep a basket of slippers near the bed for easy reach on a cold morning.

RIGHT *A seasonal change of bed linens is easy when working from a well organized closet or cabinet.*

ABOVE *Quirky but practical furniture and accessories add warmth and originality to a utilitarian room. Increased storage space makes a welcome bonus.*

OPPOSITE *A shared bath benefits from a roomy cabinet built for two. Easy-to-clean glass shelves in a recessed niche display favorite perfumes, lotions, and bath salts.*

furnishing the bathroom

Although the bathroom has always been one of the most frequently used rooms of the house, it was, in decades past, primarily a utilitarian space. A few towel bars, a basic medicine cabinet, a soap dish, and a water glass to hold toothbrushes were considered adequate furnishings. But as the demand has grown for bathrooms as luxurious retreats, and as once-simple bathing rituals have developed into product-laden procedures, bathrooms have grown bigger and more complex in their storage needs and organizational challenges.

For a bathroom to be relaxing, even spalike, it has to be organized. All the soaps and scrubs, lotions and creams, toiletries and towels used in the modern bathroom cry out for attractive containers. Before looking for these, however, consider adding a few pieces of functional furniture. These will enhance both the order and the look of the bathroom. Once organized, it is essential for the users to establish some positive habits to keep it that way. Finally, when the seasons change, so should some aspects of the bathroom. Practicality teamed with indulgence will create a bathroom that both functions and pampers.

Functional Furniture

Carefully chosen furniture can add the luxury of comfort and increased storage to even the smallest bathroom. Just one morning of trying to balance a coffee cup on the edge of the sink, only to knock it over with the hair dryer cord, dramatically illustrates the usefulness of a small table set sink-side. A slim chair or stool tucked next to the bathtub can hold a telephone, books and magazines, or even a glass of wine during a long soak.

When space is limited, bathroom furniture can do double duty. A dresser top displays things you want seen—a pitcher of flowers and guest soaps and towels—while its drawers hide what you'd prefer to leave unseen—cleaning supplies, refills for a soap dispenser, or children's bathtub toys. If there's enough room for a comfortable chair, it can provide a place to cool down after a shower or a place to sit and relax while enjoying a facial mask. Use a counter-height stool as a footrest for polishing toenails or a place to sit while applying makeup.

To avoid damage from a bathroom's frequently moist air, don't bring in fine antiques or other valuable furniture. Wicker, painted or distressed pieces, or metal furniture is best. Vintage garden furniture like side tables, folding chairs with slatted wood seats, or antique plant stands, makes perfect sense in this humid environment. The peeling paint and bits of rust only look better with age.

Other furnishing suggestions:

■ Use a ladderback chair to hold a portable CD player and headphones on the seat plus folded towels on the back's horizontal rails.

■ Give new life to an old upholstered chair by slip-covering it in white toweling trimmed with a colorful welt. If there is enough space, a wicker lounge chair or chaise lounge will give the room the feel of a luxury spa.

■ Place an unused night table from a bedroom set between the toilet and the sink to add both display and storage space.

■ Slide a long table with one or two lower shelves under a bank of windows or against an expanse of wall. Stack neatly folded bath towels on the lower shelves; reserve the top for a small lamp, hand towels, a tray of favorite perfumes, and a plant.

■ Lean a library ladder against a wall for hanging towels.

■ Without conveniently located hooks, robes tend to end up crammed onto towel bars or in a heap on the floor. Hooks are simple to install; place them where they'll be simple to use.

■ Keep lidded boxes or baskets of bath supplies handy by placing them on an étagère or small-scale baker's rack.

■ Add shelves to the interior of a vintage pie safe. The pierced metal or screen mesh front creates storage space with good air circulation.

■ Small lamps make better, and prettier, nightlights than most plug-in units sold for that purpose.

■ Use a small vintage rug instead of a bathmat. Play up the fact that this space, too, is a "living" room.

Medicine Cabinets

Medicine cabinets are about as functional as furnishings get. Because it stores most of our health and beauty essentials, an organized medicine cabinet is a bathroom priority. If it looks attractive—inside as well as out—keeping it orderly will be easier and pleasanter.

ABOVE *Slender cabinets on casters can take advantage of unused bathroom corners. Flea market finds, such as a footed fruit bowl, will add particular charm as well as a spot for scented soaps.*

You can upgrade your medicine cabinet without undertaking a full bathroom redo. Home improvement stores carry a wide array of inexpensive and utilitarian cabinets. Most are designed to be recessed into a wall, so if you're replacing your current cabinet with one the same size, you should be able to do the work yourself. However, if you want a larger size, call a contractor.

Aside from spatial constraints, there is no reason that each member of the family cannot have his or her own medicine

INSPIRATION FROM THE PAST

The idea of incorporating furniture into the bathroom is not new. Many decades before the reign of all-tile-and-porcelain bathrooms, some prominent style setters filled their bathrooms with functional furniture and creative storage solutions.

- Elsie de Wolfe, who gave birth to the decorating profession in the early 1900s, furnished the bathroom of her Paris apartment as she would any other room. De Wolfe would receive and entertain friends in her bath salon while touching up her makeup or sprawling on the settee. Her salon du bain was the talk of Paris and often imitated in both Europe and the United States.

- In their Paris home, the Duke and Duchess of Windsor had bathrooms so elaborate and handsomely furnished, they could double as sitting rooms. Although the duke had a desk in the dressing area off his bathroom, he apparently needed additional workspace, for he covered the tub with a large piece of wood to create a place for books and papers. Beneath the wooden slab, the tub was filled with file boxes. Apparently he was a shower man.

- David Hicks, the late British designer whose ideas are enjoying a resurgence in popularity, wrote, "Bathrooms should be furnished, comfortable, and welcoming places." In the last years of his life, he incorporated bathroom facilities directly into his country house bedroom. The bathtub sat in an alcove between two closets, and the sink was set into the top of a bookcase underneath a window. Round mirrors on extendable arms were mounted on the woodwork beside the window so as not to block the garden view.

CREATIVE CONTAINERS

Keeping the bathroom organized is an easier and more enjoyable task if you search out attractive containers and accessories. Don't limit yourself to items found in bath shops; instead, think about using pottery, glassware, silver, and other pieces in unexpected ways.

- Display a collection of colorful pottery vases, cups, and bowls and use them to hold makeup brushes, cotton balls, and hair accessories.

- Why settle for a boring toothbrush holder? Depending on your bathroom's decor, consider using a Mexican green glass tumbler, a small silver trophy, or a rustic earthenware mug.

- A footed glass candy dish makes a perfect soap holder, as does an antique teacup saucer.

- Organize an assortment of perfume bottles, lipsticks, or bath gels by grouping them on a tray. Suitable tray choices are plentiful: silver, Japanese lacquer, woven wire, or even a large square glass platter.

- In a rustic bathroom, large earthenware bowls look handsome when filled with soaps, hand towels, and sea sponges.

- Hanging wall baskets can hold makeup, bath products, or a small hairdryer. Or borrow a space-saving idea from hotels and store your hairdryer in a cloth pouch hung from a wall hook.

- Roll up towels and place them in a large basket, set on the floor, to free up cabinet space.

cabinet. This is especially helpful when there is only one bathroom and the entire family gets ready for work and school at the same time. Hang kids' cabinets lower for easy access.

Whether you are adding a new cabinet or just sprucing up the one you already have, here are ways to make your medicine cabinet more decorative and user-friendly:

- Dress up the front of the medicine cabinet with an art glass mirror.

- Use mirrors on both sides of medicine cabinet doors.

- Use removable glass shelves. They are easier to clean than metal or wood.

- Get rid of unsightly containers. Use glass bottles with cork stoppers or pump dispensers to decant everything from mouthwash and moisturizer to aspirin and facial toner.

- Paste self-adhesive labels to the bottom of the bottles and label the contents. Store the remaining contents in a hall closet and refill your decorative bottles as needed.

- Glue thin-ply cork used for bulletin boards to the inside. Pin inspirational quotes here or directions for your latest skin care program. This mini-bulletin board is also a great place to post love notes to a spouse or a note that says, "I'm proud of you" to a child.

- Customize his and her cabinets. For his, include an electric outlet for recharging an electric razor. For hers, use a thick piece of Plexiglas for one shelf with cut holes in it to hold makeup brushes and lipsticks.

LEFT *Even behind-doors storage can give visual pleasure when the contents are organized into neat groups and interesting containers. Casual enamelware buckets and bowls, purloined from the kitchen, provide crisp, clean container alternatives.*

- Try some alternatives to the standard medicine cabinet. A small wall-hung cabinet originally designed for kitchen storage can be just as useful in the bathroom. The same goes for plate racks or bookshelves.

- If your bathroom is wallpapered, use the same wallpaper inside the medicine cabinet as well. Or, for the ultimate in medicine cabinet interiors, take inspiration from the artist who painted hers to depict rooms in a dollhouse. The top shelf was the attic with storage trunks and toys. The middle showed a bedroom and bathroom. The lower shelf was the kitchen, entryway, and living room. What child—or grown-up—wouldn't be inspired to keep that cabinet organized?

Guest Bathrooms

"Spend a night in your own guest room" is oft-repeated advice, but you should also spend time in your own guest bathroom. Is there sufficient lighting for applying makeup? Are towels within easy reach of tub or shower? Is there a handy hook for a robe?

Keep the interior of the medicine cabinet and drawers as tidy as the rest of the room. If a guest needs an aspirin, he shouldn't have to search through half-used tubes of toothpaste, dull disposable razors, and other bathroom detritus, nor should he discover drawers filled with out-of-date cosmetics or skin medication. Use some of the cabinet and drawer space for fresh bars of soap, new disposable razors, a full box of tissues, and small, unopened containers of shampoo and body lotion.

One of the best things you can provide for your guests, however, is some empty space, not only in the medicine cabinet and drawers, but also on the vanity top. Guest bathrooms tend to attract decorative knick-knacks. Keep these to a minimum. A basket piled with fresh hand towels will be appreciated far more than a dried flower arrangement or a tray of ancient, half-evaporated bottles of perfume.

Just before guests arrive, check to see that fresh towels, new bars of soap (or freshly filled liquid soap containers), and a big bath mat are in place. Then, if the room has a bathtub/shower combination, take one more second and tuck the shower curtain liner inside the tub. Many guests don't check this until the shower is spraying water onto the bathroom floor.

Nice additions:

- Jars of cotton balls, cotton swabs, and disposable makeup sponges;

- Clearly labeled bottles of bath and shower gel;

- Travel-size bottles of hand lotion and mouthwash;

- Emergency fix-its: clear nail polish for hosiery snags and a small sewing kit;

- A freestanding magnifying mirror, or, even more luxurious, a wall-mounted magnifying mirror with built-in light;

- A high-powered hair dryer;

- Terry-cloth robes;

- A handheld clothes steamer.

OPPOSITE *Lockerlike cabinetry, a bevy of baskets, and expansive shelving allow for easy and effective organization of a busy family bathroom.*

positive household habits

- Wiping out the sink and straightening the counter top after every use leaves the bathroom organized and attractive for the next user. Small messes left behind expand exponentially with each additional user.

- After using a hairdryer or electric razor, return it immediately to its designated cabinet or drawer. This takes only a second and prevents an ugly tangle of cords. A curling iron may need a few minutes to cool but also should be stored as soon as possible.

- Make hanging up wet towels so convenient that no one has an excuse for leaving them in a soggy heap on the floor. If wall-hung towel bars are not accomplishing that goal, add one or more of the following:

  ❖ A standing blanket or quilt rack

  ❖ A wooden valet stand

  ❖ A wooden board mounted with Shaker-style pegs

  ❖ A bar or ring mounted on each end of the vanity

  ❖ A freestanding heated chrome towel rack

- Keep only the gels and lotions you use daily out. Displaying colorful bottles of pampering potions is fine, but a waste of space if never used. A small vase of flowers or a potted orchid would be a better decorative choice.

- Devote some decluttering time to the linen closet. Throw away threadbare towels and washcloths. If you think some day you'll use them as cleaning rags, move them to the laundry room supply closet or garage.

ABOVE, TOP *Freshly laundered towels, rolled and packed into a deep basket with sturdy handles, can be easily transported from the top of the dryer to the side of the bathtub.*

ABOVE, BOTTOM *An unusual assemblage of silver serving pieces and vintage cosmetic containers calm potential countertop chaos. Flea markets and antique collectives are filled with such finds.*

Seasonal Changes

When the Air Is Warm

- Change bath accessories. Stick to light-colored towels and put the dark ones away for the season. Change soap dispensers and dishes, water tumblers, and toothbrush holders to add bright splashes of color. Try an awning-striped shower curtain; it's like stepping in and out of a beach cabana.

- Replace bathmats with inexpensive sisal rugs. The tropical look will counter the heat outside.

- Lighten the fragrances—potpourri, soaps, lotions, and room sprays—to reflect the season. In winter, rich fragrances like sandalwood, pine, and eucalyptus are welcome. In the spring, lighten up with fruit scents like lemon, lime, and pear, or with florals like gardenia, freesia, rose, and lilac.

- Move the scale out of winter storage to monitor your bikini weight.

- Keep beach towels handy, ready for summer fun. Hang them on towel bars to remind you to head to the beach as often as possible.

- Put up removable hooks with suction backs to provide a place for wet bathing suits to dry.

- Put a removable strainer in your shower drain to catch sand.

- Check expiration dates and contents of sunscreen tubes before departing on vacation. The stores near your exotic resort may not carry your favorites.

- Place postcards of tropical destinations in your medicine cabinet to remind you what summer is all about: relaxation and sun.

When the Air Is Cool

- Move all evidence of summer, like beach towels and bathing caps, to storage. But keep a note in your household journal of where you put them. A winter vacation to warm weather spots may be a surprise Christmas gift.

- Exchange whiter-than-white towels for softer colors like bone and khaki. Just a subtle change in color will signify a change in the season.

- Use dense pile bathmats. They envelop the feet in warmth.

- Check the expiration dates on medications. Throw out those that have outlived their potency.

- Buy scented candles that remind you of trees like pine and spruce. It's amazing how a simple scent can trigger memories of a cozy country weekend.

- Use earthenware and raku pottery as soap dishes and to hold towels and sponges. Add pumice stones and loofahs to scrub away winter's dry, rough skin.

- Have self-heating massage oil handy to warm cold, tired limbs.

- Keep chamomile tea bags in a glass jar by the bath. Infuse your steaming hot bath with relaxing herbs.

- Look for bath gels in colors like amber and dark whiskey. Warm colors trigger a feeling of well-being.

ABOVE *A rustic oak stool makes a handy perch for people, stacks of fresh towels, or a woven wicker basket of sea sponges.*

RIGHT *Small, wall-mounted storage cabinets free up floor space in a compact contemporary powder room.*

Powder Rooms: Fantasies and Realities

Do you hang fancy little linen guest towels in the powder room? Most need so much starch to look fresh that they barely absorb enough water to dry anyone's hands and then turn unattractively crumpled after a single use. Do you also have a container of paper hand towels on the counter, signaling: "Please don't touch the fancy ones"?

Why not discard the fantasy that you dwell in a manor house staffed with a full-time laundress and be realistic? Send the fancy little towels off to a charity resale shop, and use the towel bar to hang some interesting reading material, perhaps a copy of *Paris Match* or the *New York Times Magazine*. Better still, remove the towel bar altogether and blanket the wall with art or a collection of vintage mirrors. (If some of the linen towels are too beautiful to discard, frame them in shadowboxes and hang them on the wall.)

Stack good-looking paper hand towels in a shallow basket or on a narrow silver tray. For a big party, borrow an idea from luxury hotels and stock up on inexpensive small white washcloths from a discount store, roll them into neat little cylinders, and stand them on end in a deep basket. Place another basket on the floor near the cabinet for used cloths. Put one cloth in the "used" basket to give guests a guide.

Slimy, half-used bars of soap have no place in an organized powder room. Either use an attractive pump dispenser of liquid soap or provide small use-once-and-discard guest soaps. Display individual soaps in small tureens: ones with missing lids work fine and are less expensive at flea markets and antique collectives.

If the powder room gets infrequent family use, be sure to make a quick pre-party check that the hot water runs hot, the cold water doesn't dislodge bits of rust, and the toilet flushes effectively. And although extra rolls of toilet paper should be easy to find, they shouldn't be perched in plain sight. Store them in a lidded basket or inside a cabinet.

taming children's rooms

Children's rooms are their personal havens. While adults have dominion over the whole house, kids have only their little slices of space. A child's room is, in a sense, his world. When planning a child's room, beware of dictating your ideas or attempting to create the room you never had. Make your child's room unique to his or her own needs, interests, and—yes, even at a very young age—personal tastes.

Of course you can guide children, but help them to reach at least some of the decisions themselves. Ask questions. Even a three-year-old knows what colors he loves or hates. A school-age child can have strong ideas about where the bed should be located in the room. Her sibling may be equally opinionated on how she keeps and displays her favorite collection.

Why invest in a piece of furniture your children don't even want? Your ten-year-old son may prefer an old teak deck chair to his grandpa's hand-me-down rocker. A young girl may long for a drop-front secretary with lots of nooks and shelves for her treasures and trinkets rather than a more traditional desk. An artistic teenager might prefer a drafting table instead of a writing desk. Children will be more vested in keeping the room relatively tidy when they've made some of the design choices themselves, no matter how minor.

In planning for a child's room, start with a function-based layout. Designate areas for sleeping and dressing, working and playing. Once you break down the floor plan into activity areas, you can maximize each section's efficiency and storage capacity by means of furniture and container choices.

Finally, some thoughts on theme rooms: Confine a theme to elements that can be changed easily as children grow and passions for particular favorites fade. Convey a circus theme, for example, with fabric pennants tacked to the walls and colorful, inexpensive reproductions of circus posters rather than with an elaborate hand-painted mural. Then, when the child tires of the Big Top decor, all the elements are easily removed and discarded, and the next theme can take its place.

Be particularly careful about investing in major furniture pieces that are theme-related. Resist the urge to buy a train-loving toddler a bed in the shape of a locomotive or a little girl an armoire elaborately hand-painted with scenes of fairy princesses. All too soon the toddler can turn his affections from trains to racing cars, or the girl can decide that princesses are passé.

OPPOSITE *A whimsical pink and red wardrobe with big purple door pulls makes putting away clothes more fun than a chore. The cheery coverlet, in a bright rainbow of coordinating stripes, simplifies bed making even for the preschool set.*

Functional Furniture

Beds. A day bed offers a sofalike look and is perfect for toddler and teenager alike. Use the space underneath for a trundle bed or removable storage baskets or drawers. Invest in a good bed frame, something appealing like painted iron, wicker, or hardwood. Choose a classic style; it may end up in your office or guest room some day.

To make the area under the bed even more useful, purchase just a mattress and build a base to hold it at whatever height and width the storage situation requires. You can outfit the space underneath with shelves or leave it open to house bulky camping or sports equipment. If you'd rather avoid carpentry completely, use sturdy storage cubes as the mattress base.

In a small room, borrow an idea from college dormitories and raise the bed high enough to leave room for a study area below. Or hang a curtain along the base of the raised bed to create a closet or play space underneath the sleeping nook.

Bunk beds are useful when siblings share a room. If turf wars are frequent, creating a barrackslike room, complete with footlockers or dressers at each side of the bunks, may be the only way to delineate the space. Bunk beds also give a child a place for a friend to sleep over or just to switch his own sleeping spot occasionally.

Desks. Kids need generously sized desks, not the small writing desks that permeate the market today. Schoolwork and hobbies quickly render a small desktop filled and useless. Instead, buy them adult-sized desks that have adjustable bases so the desks can grow with them. Put computer printers and scanners on a rolling cart or small table next to the desk to save desktop space. A file cabinet on wheels would work well too.

Night Tables. Children love to have things—lots of things—by their beds. Don't fight it. It may be a collection of comforting stuffed animals, the latest video game release, or simply pictures of friends. A roomy nightstand can hold a lot on top and in drawers. Small dressers work wonders, or a cluster of four stacking cubbies can also provide enough room for a child's bedside treasures.

Chests. Don't waste money buying a traditional changing table for a nursery. Instead, invest in a sturdy low bureau and top it with a plastic pad with a terry cloth cover. Store diapers, pins, and ointments in the drawers beneath. When diaper days are past, the room still has a useful storage piece.

Toy boxes and blanket chests make good foot-of-the-bed containers to hold shoes, sweatshirts, or heavy sweaters. Or tuck a toy box under a window to make an instant window seat.

Seating. Even a baby's room needs an adult-size chair. A comfortable armchair or rocking chair is good for the early months of feeding, and then, in later years, for book reading. If the room is large enough, a chaise lounge is a smart choice and can provide an extra sleeping spot for a visiting chum. A built-in window seat with storage underneath is another desirable addition to a child's bedroom.

Mirrors. Although shops offer a variety of child-appropriate small mirrors for bureau tops or walls, make sure there is at least one full-length mirror in the room. As kids get older and become more concerned with their appearance, their own ample mirror will help keep them from occupying the family bathroom for hours on end.

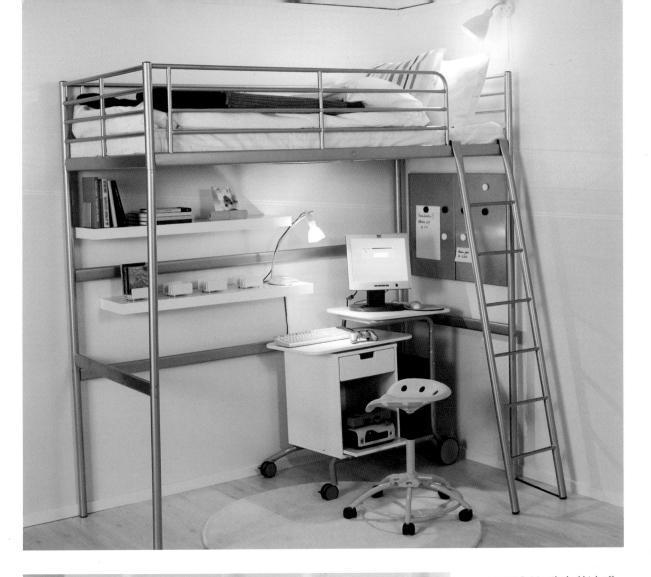

ABOVE *Raising the bed high off the floor in a teenager's bedroom frees space underneath for a study area outfitted with a computer station on casters. A bright yellow stool, reminiscent of a tractor seat, adds a jaunty touch.*

LEFT *A coat of paint turns an inexpensive table and chair set into pretty-in-pink furnishings for a little girl's play corner. Baskets or bins spray painted the same deep pink color would help identify storage for art supplies, tea sets, and other toys to be used at the table.*

CRAFT AN ART AREA

If you designate a specific section of a child's room as the place for doing art work, constructing craft projects, or even conducting tea parties, you're less likely to find crayons, glue sticks, and cookie crumbs scattered throughout the rest of the room. Some suggestions for what to include:

- A table the appropriate height for the child,

- A pair of child-sized chairs, plus some adult-sized seating, if only a big pillow on the floor,

- A bookshelf lined with storage bins for craft supplies,

- An easel and smock (an old adult-size T-shirt makes a terrific child's smock),

- An enormous blackboard,

- A sheet of vinyl flooring to cover carpet and wood floors and protect them from stray bits of paint, glue, and clay,

- A large, colorful trash can.

ABOVE *A bright yellow rolling cart provides an appealing storage spot for art and craft supplies. A budding artist can move it next to a table while creating, then, later, scoot it out of the way. A big blue wastebasket helps with cleaning up.*

Storage Solutions

Clothing. Small children don't need a lot of hanging space in their closets. So many of their clothes store just fine when folded that it makes sense to keep only one small pole for hanging and convert the rest of the closet to shelves. If closet space is at a premium or nonexistent, an armoire works well to keep clothes organized.

If you find your children constantly draping clothes over chairs, bed, or floor, add coat racks or antique hall trees to their rooms. Convince them that slinging a sweatshirt over a hook is only minimally more demanding than dropping it on a chair.

A coat rack or hall tree is just a start. Children's rooms can benefit from as many hooks as you can find hanging places.

Each large hook can hold several items. Look for simple metal schoolhouse-style hooks, contemporary stainless steel hooks, porcelain towel hooks rescued from a bathroom remodel, or Shaker-style wooden pegs.

If even the handsomest and handiest hooks are ignored (Welcome to the teen years!) at least place a sturdy, extra-large basket near the bedroom door so book bags, athletic shoes, and other paraphernalia can be confined to a single spot.

Toys. Most children have far too many toys. Their rooms are crammed with stuffed animals and packed with plastic creations ranging from miniature cars to multistory dollhouses. Too often it all verges on sensory overload, to say nothing of creating colossal clutter. Baskets, bins, crates, and buckets are wonderful for toy storage, but continually buying more containers is not the answer.

First, try to control the supply sources. Gently suggest that relatives and friends give gifts that do not add to the toy tsunami. Why not a trip to the zoo instead of yet another stuffed animal, or some shiny silver dollars for a piggy bank rather than another doll? For an older child, a savings bond could be the start of a fund to purchase a bicycle or other coveted major item.

Next, limit the number of toys a child has access to at any given time. Pack some away to bring out later, when they will be greeted like old friends. This will help not only with the clutter issue but with cleaning up as well.

Once you have reduced the toy population, it's time to consider containers. Tiny toys can be stored in large plastic jars so the contents are visible. A multicompartment fabric shoe bag, hung from a closet doorknob or special peg, can hold favorite small stuffed animals, toy cars, or found treasures. Even a very young child can manage to return toys to these handy compartments. A sand pail can hold rubber toys for the child to tote to bath time. But baskets or bins—wicker, metal, or plastic—are the containers most likely to save your sanity and reduce room-cleanup drama. Line them up on a low shelf, a long table, or simply on the floor along a wall or under a window. When the child gets older, these same containers can hold magazines, books, small sports equipment, photo albums, CDs, DVDs, and computer games.

It's far easier to tidy a child's room when all the child (or you) have to do is sweep piles of playthings into waiting containers. If the containers then make their way to shelves or closet space, the room can't help but look organized.

Curating and Displaying Children's Collections

Kids are inveterate collectors, but in the organized home, a little parental curating is necessary. First, confine the great majority of children's collections to their own rooms. Otherwise, a river of seashells, rocks, airplane models, dolls, or whatever will run rampant through the entire house.

Next, establish a rule that when a multitude of new items arrive, some older ones must leave; but let the child decide what has to go. Don't try to secretly remove items. Kids always know immediately when something is missing.

Once the ready-for-departure items have been chosen, their destination can be a clearly marked box in a storage space, a friend's room—although this will win you no friendship points with the pal's parents—a children's ward at a local hospital, or a charity resale shop. As attractive a choice as the trash bin may seem, this disposal method requires extreme tact—or dark of night—and isn't really fair play.

Built-in shelves, freestanding bookcases, and small cabinets are among the easiest ways to create display space in a child's room. If the room is small, hang cabinets or individual cubbies from the wall to keep as much floor space as possible free for playing.

OPPOSITE *Narrow shelves mounted on the wall near the crafts corner of a child's bedroom make an ideal display area for art works and favorite photographs.*

For artwork, posters, postcards, and similar collections, an immense bulletin board does the job. For children just past toddler stage, consider using a metal bulletin board with large magnets instead of cork or other material that would require pushpins or thumbtacks. Easy-to-hang plastic shadowboxes are another alternative, and, for older children, clip-glass frames make it simple to change artwork on a whim.

Somewhat battered vintage suitcases often can be had for a song at flea markets and tag sales. Fill them with a child's collectibles and stack them in a corner, adding storage and a hint of nostalgia to the room.

ABOVE *Seashells and rocks. Monsters and magic tricks. Bird nests and bugs. All the treasures toted home in a child's jeans pocket stay orderly and accessible in clearly labeled plastic boxes housed in an open wood cabinet.*

ABOVE *Simple iron bed frames create a nostalgic mood in this shared bedroom. Bed coverings are kept simple, with no fussy dust ruffles to impede access to the big wicker storage boxes that slide out easily from under the beds. A massive chest with hinged lid serves as a toy box, and a smaller chest on wheels acts as a bedside table. Four twelve-inch (30.5 cm)-square panels attached to the wall and bordered with apple green paint create a witty full-length mirror.*

positive household habits

If making the bed is easy, a child may do it more regularly. Keep bedding uncomplicated: simple sheets and a comforter or lightweight bedspread that can be pulled up with minimal effort. Once the bed is made, positive reinforcement is key. Give fulsome praise for sincere efforts, and even if it's all a bit lumpy; don't remake the bed to your standard! Children pick up on these not-so-subtle signals that tell them they have failed, or worse, that you'll remake it anyway, so why bother?

For young children, have a silly song you sing when it's time to clean up a play area and put craft supplies and toys away. It's a fun way to lure them into this sometimes balked-at task.

Include a few plants in the child's room, both as decorative accents and as an incentive for learning responsibility. Even a twelve-year-old boy can learn to love and nurture a cactus or two.

Ban snacks and soft drinks from children's rooms from the first day they can understand the phrase "Let's have our cookies at the kitchen table" right up through the times they sulk when told "No pizza parties in your bedroom." You will, at times, be labeled controlling and unloving. Your children's rooms, however, will be a lot cleaner.

When dealing with a truly horrific room inhabited by a teenager, simply shutting the door between the onset of puberty and the beginning of freshman year in college is probably the best policy. Unable to bear the knowledge of the chaos behind the closed door? Then negotiate minimal room maintenance standards upon which the continuance of the teen's allowance, driving privileges, and the like, will depend. And, good luck.

OPPOSITE *A yellow-and-white-check blanket lies across the foot of a bunk bed, ready to supplement the colorful quilt on the first cold night. Set up for siblings to share, the room uses wall-mounted desks with sconces above to create compact desk space.*

Seasonal Changes

When the Air Is Warm

- Put winter clothes in storage, weeding out items that no longer fit.

- Designate a closet spot for swimsuits, day camp T-shirts, or any other summer garb likely to be needed at a moment's notice.

- Change the room layout so the bed is closer to a window for fresh air.

- Clean air ducts if your child is prone to allergies.

When the Air Is Cool

- Clear a shelf in the closet for heavy sweaters and scarves.

- Lay an extra blanket across the foot of the bed.

- Up the wattage on light bulbs as sunny hours diminish.

- Toys can be seasonal too. Put away summer sports equipment, pool toys, and beach pails and shovels; bring out the wintertime board games and puzzles.

making the home office work

Your home office should be highly personal as well as highly productive. If it's attractive, you'll enjoy spending time in it, and if it's efficient, you'll be more productive.

Start with a functional floor plan, taking into account the way you actually work and how you like to store work-related materials. Perhaps you need shelves to hold three-ring binders or shallow drawers to hold drawings more than you need multiple deep file drawers. If you spend hours at the computer keyboard, then a comfortable ergonomic chair will be key. If you meet with clients in your home office, you need an attractive, comfortable seating area. You may even want to include a small day bed for an occasional nap; after all, one of the advantages of working at home is the ability to establish your own schedule.

Once you've identified the room's functional needs, you can turn your attention to other practical, yet stylish furnishings, such as extra tables, good-looking cabinets, and innovative bulletin boards. Too often, home offices are decor impaired. Boring furniture, electronic equipment with its tangle of cords, cardboard boxes of supplies, and a plethora of papers, pamphlets, books, and mail all combine to create an area sorely in need of aesthetic as well as functional organization. When you get your office both organized and attractive, a few good habits will help maintain order and make your home office work for you.

OPPOSITE *An entire office wall given over to storage means files and other reference materials are just a glance away from the work area. Here, a dining table does desk duty, and a handsome leather side chair is a decorative alternative to an office supply store model.*

ABOVE *Two legal-sized file cabinets topped with a wooden counter create generous storage capability as well as a spacious surface for laying out project materials. An old wooden frame with a new coat of paint and a metal sheet cut to size make a handy memo board.*

Functional Furniture

Resist cookie-cutter office furniture that looks as if it belongs in a boardroom rather than a home. When a space is personal and furniture is interesting, you will get a lot of pleasure from its use. If your office starts as a hodgepodge of cast-off furniture and well-worn file cabinets, change it into a cohesive group by painting everything the same color—perhaps black, white, mossy green, or even vermilion. Color unites.

Desks. Although a wealth of modern desk styles are available from office furniture manufacturers, there are also wonderful vintage pieces out there. If you find a desk you love and a few drawers are missing, just use baskets in their place or keep the spaces as easy-access storage cubbies. A worn top can be covered with leather, copper, zinc, or even a thick Navaho blanket, which provides a nicely padded surface.

Other possibilities from the antique collective or consignment store:

- A pine dining table;

- A turn-of-the-century kitchen table with pull-out flour bins, which can hold files or supplies;

- An antique partners' desk for a shared office;

- A round oak library table for an office with a bay window.

In fact, almost any desk looks great set against a window. You have to decide if the view will delight or distract you.

For a more contemporary feel, try a pair of two-drawer file cabinets topped with a wooden door. Although it may be a budget-desk cliché, variations on this serviceable concept can look terrific. Consider black file cabinets topped with an expanse of gleaming birch, a length of black laminate, or a piece of butcher block. Metal file cabinets from flea markets and resale shops are very inexpensive. Spray paint them yourself, or take them to an auto body shop.

A variation on this concept is a shelflike desktop installed along the length of a wall with file cabinets on casters underneath. Keep the file cabinets under the desk until needed. If you have a lot of filing to do, move a cabinet next to a comfortable chair.

Triple the workspace of a freestanding desk by floating it in mid-room and surrounding it with wood-topped file cabinets. Or, steal an idea from the kitchen and supplement the desk with a central island. This could be a simple round table, a long, narrow refectory-style table, or even a slab of plywood with steel file cabinets as supports. An island is ideal for ongoing-project materials: a place to arrange color or fabric samples, sort multipage documents, or lay out open reference books.

Tables. A small, sturdy table standing idle in another part of the house should be commandeered for office use. Placed next to the desk or a bookcase, a little table will prove endlessly useful. Rolling tables are particularly handy. Combine two of them to make one large table for a project, or separate them to make individual workstations for temporary helpers. Even an easy-to-move vintage drinks cart can serve as a laptop computer table to use next to your desk for some projects and then move alongside an easy chair for others. Other useful and interesting tables for offices: a long Belgian baker's table, a stainless metal table from a restaurant kitchen, or a battered old rectangular table spruced up with a tailored canvas skirt.

Chairs. A desk chair is a very personal choice; use what is comfortable for you. Perhaps one of your dining room chairs fills the bill, or an old Windsor chair handed down through generations of family members will give your office a personal touch. A rolling wooden chair from the 1940s or '50s, rescued from a flea market and given a bright coat of paint, can add a quirky note to your home office, while an armless leather chair with classical lines will add an element of elegance.

ABOVE *The quirky corner of an attic office makes visual and functional sense when fitted with a built-in daybed. A collection of baskets takes advantage of the storage space created below the bed.*

A banker's swivel chair, either new or reclaimed, is easy to pull up to a pocket-sized office created within a closet. Hanging file pockets take advantage of space on the inside of a door. Flanking storage shelves can be curtained off when not in use.

The advantage of a chair from an office furnishings source, however, is its ability to be set to the ideal height for your desktop. Look for one that provides good support for your back and arms and a footrest to relieve leg pressure. If you choose a chair without a built-in footrest, use a small footstool during long sessions at the computer. A rolling chair is perfect if you shift frequently between work areas. But don't limit the chair's upholstery to institutional gray. Make a personal decorative statement by reupholstering it in a yellow and white toile, supple chestnut-brown leather, or a businesslike navy wool pinstripe.

Cabinets. Cabinet pieces originally designed for other areas of the house can make effective office storage pieces. Consider:

- A pine hutch,

- Salvaged wardrobe cabinets,

- A dry sink—perfect for holding a copier—with space below for copy paper and other supplies,

- Baker's racks,

- Metal medical cabinets,

- Metro industrial shelves.

Day Beds. A day bed not only can serve as a place for a quick nap or another place for a guest to sit or spend the night, but, in a room where sometimes every available space must be pulled into use, its large surface is perfect for sorting paperwork, laying out samples, or organizing receipts.

You can fashion a day bed from a twin box spring and mattress mounted on a simple frame and covered with layers of quilts and vintage pillows or seek out a turn-of-the-century iron day bed with a well worn patina. Even a twin bed with a wood or upholstered headboard and footboard could do the job, or a single bed from a suite of Victorian-era furniture.

Flat Files. You don't have to be an architect, engineer, or professional artist to find storage nirvana with flat files. These large cabinets with stacks of shallow drawers come in a variety of sizes and finishes, in both wood and steel. Install one on the optional raised base to provide room for lidded baskets or small, portable boxes underneath, or stand several side-by-side to create a sleek, contemporary look. Flat files not only provide organized storage space but also create a generous table surface if placed in the center of the room.

RIGHT *Be on the lookout for containers in unexpected places, and, when you find them, buy them in groups of three or more. Here, glazed flowerpots hold pencils, pens, and a folding ruler, as well as an ivy plant.*

Vintage variations on the flat file model are challenging to locate but look so interesting, while storing so much, that a search is worthwhile. An old map case, a print cabinet, or even an antique linen press will give an office both organizational space and style.

Customized Closets

An office closet tends to breed chaos. Whether you install a system of shelves and cubbies, stack file cabinets in the space, or even outfit it with kitchen cabinets purchased from a salvage store, you should give a closet some sort of organizational structure. Vinyl-coated wire pullout shelves designed for kitchen pantries can also hold office supplies. Hanging a five-pocket metal file holder on the inside of the closet door will keep current files handy.

Another alternative is to use the interior of a closet to house all your electronic equipment, such as a printer, fax, copier, and so on. It may take some specialty wiring by a professional, but keeping oversized and boring-but-essential equipment out of sight keeps the room visually appealing.

BULLETIN BOARDS

Bulletin boards serve as memo locations and art displays, while adding a level of texture to the room. When planning a bulletin board, remember: Bigger is better, and huge is most helpful of all. Create a board that complements your office decor by using:

- A zinc or stainless steel panel with small round magnets;

- Black or taupe canvas stapled tautly over the entire wall area left between a long desktop and the bottom of an overhanging shelf, the canvas's raw edges finished with ribbon.;

- A large easel holding a piece of plaster-board wrapped in fabric, perhaps thin red wool or nubby gray tweed;

- A closet door exterior painted with black or green chalkboard paint;

- A large piece of plywood covered with cork and framed with molding that echoes the molding in the room;

- An entire wall covered in cork or uphol-stered. What could be better than a floor-to-ceiling bulletin board?

LEFT *Small decorative touches can have a big impact, even in an office. Lipstick red accents, from the bulletin board ribbons and stacking boxes to the chair upholstery and wastebasket, draw your eye away from the functional but boring beige office equipment.*

SMALL ADDITIONS WITH BIG BENEFITS

Power up the office with some of the following ergonomically savvy products.

- A split keyboard takes some time to get used to but will help prevent the wrist and arm pain that can result from repetitive stress injury. Gel wrist packs also reduce the risk of injury from long periods at the computer.

- A headset for the telephone will save on the neck strain that results from cradling a receiver against your shoulder. Attach a small hook on the side of the desk to hold the headset when not in use.

- If you spend much time drawing or writing by hand, an inclined work surface will reduce neck pressure and eyestrain. Inexpensive drafting tables are available at art supply stores.

- Place the computer monitor on a swing arm attached to the wall if desktop space is limited. Pivoting pullout keyboard drawers make use of awkward corners.

- Before plugging in all your electronic equipment, add a surge protector: one of the best home office investments you can make. For under $50 you can prevent an electrical surge from zapping your computer or frying your fax machine.

Containing the Chaos

In the home office, containers are important keys to maintaining organization. Use any kind of container that works while also looking attractive: wire or woven wicker baskets, fabric-covered boxes, or antique hat boxes are just a few of the myriad of possibilities. When you find baskets or boxes you like, buy a lot of them; matching pieces give storage shelves a streamlined look. But be careful about loading the desktop with too many small baskets, lest they turn this important work area into a clutter bin. It's generally best to limit desktop baskets to two: one "in" basket, for unopened mail, recent faxes, or e-mail printouts that need written responses, and an "out" basket for papers to be filed, recorded, or posted. Corral the rest of the desktop detritus into a small tansu, letter box, or Chinese scholar's box—all of which have drawers and cubbies that provide perfect storage for memo pads, writing tools, paper clips, and other necessities. These layered "cabinets on cabinets" are the building blocks for decorative storage.

LEFT *Shop your own attic, basement, and closets for office containers. In this bookcase, woven sea grass boxes, a large glass jar, galvanized metal buckets, an antique painted tin sewing box, and a contemporary stack of mini-drawers delight your eye as well as organize your supplies.*

OPPOSITE *Use ceiling-high shelves to capture every inch of available wall space when carving an office from an unused corner of a bedroom. Outfit the shelves with stackable boxes and bins, keeping their colors consistent with the bedroom's decor.*

If you prefer having most of your desktop paraphernalia in plain view, be creative about small containers. Pens, pencils, scissors, and the like look terrific stored in a collection of Roseville vases, wooden bowls, ceramic jars, or even recycled tin cans. A bartender's condiment box can hold paper clips, plastic file tabs, and bulletin board pushpins instead of olives, lime wedges, and candied cherries. Use your imagination.

A sterling silver toast holder, perhaps unearthed in an antique shop or from the back of your china cabinet, can be a desktop letter holder. A rustic wood tool tote could hold drawing or writing supplies and is easy to move to another work area. Even a humble saucer can hold a pile of stamps on your desk.

For major storage demands, buy metal wire racks and fill one wall with them. To keep shelves orderly, fill large cookie or spice jars with office supplies like staples, paper clips, or stamps. Clear glass jars help you see instantly what supplies need replenishing.

STEALING OFFICE SPACE

When you can't dedicate an entire room to an office space, there are plenty of other options.

- The drop-front of an antique secretary makes the perfect little space for a laptop, a notepad, and a cup of strong coffee. When work is complete, flip the desk surface back to the closed position.

- A home office within the master bedroom provides privacy and convenience, but it should not be visible from the bed. If the room's architecture doesn't include an offset nook or ell, screen off the work area with anything from a translucent Japanese screen to a custom-designed bookcase. Better yet would be taking over a closet. Popping a window into it, if at all possible, will enhance the space's visual appeal.

- Slice a section of floor space from a spare bedroom. Partition off the entire length of a twelve-foot (3.7 m) or longer wall and create two side-by-side closets, each six feet wide by two feet deep (1.8 by 0.6 m). Use one for desk and bulletin board space; outfit the other with shelves and cubbyholes. Invisible hinges on the closet doors will let the office spaces disappear at bedtime. Even during the day, you can close the doors and use the room as a yoga room or meditation space.

- Examine your home carefully for underused space. Attics, garages, and even wide stair landings can yield enough space for a well planned home office. Be imaginative when furnishing an unexpected office location. A scrounged space, such as a triangular-shaped office carved out of a part of a garage, can seem planned if the desk also has a triangular shape.

OPPOSITE *Extensive shelves built into a landing create a reference library for an adjacent home office. Broad windowsills provide spaces for leaving reference books open or displaying art objects.*

positive household habits

- Label all computer discs immediately.

- Clip, tie, or tape a label onto each computer or electrical cord so you know which is which and what is what.

- Keep business stationery sorted and ready to use. In addition to letter-size paper, have small notepads printed with your name and contact information to clip to a document you're sending to a friend or business contact.

- If you work from home, keep business bills separate from household financial papers. This keeps them safe from the prying eyes of part-time staff or helpers.

- Stock up on stamps and invest in a postage scale. Either buy plenty of stamps when at the post office or purchase your postage through the Internet. Avoid the nightmare of being up against a deadline and having to stand in a post office line.

- Buy boxes of your favorite pens so you never run out.

- Use a calligraphy font on file labels. Be creative while being organized.

Allocate a spot near the office door for items you need to take with you when you leave. This could be an empty tabletop, a large square basket, or a designated shelf in an armoire with the doors removed. Always set the items you need for a meeting, post office trip, or other errand in this spot. Then when you're ready to depart, you can scoop everything up and be off, confident you haven't forgotten anything.

OPPOSITE *An old armoire gives your office both storage space and a decorative focal point, particularly when the interior is painted a cheerful color. Even the top can hold a row of matching rustic baskets for additional storage capacity.*

taking a fresh look at laundry and mud rooms

Both laundry rooms and mud rooms pose similar organizational challenges: how to deal with items that may be soiled, wet, bulky, and unsightly and yet must be easily accessible. Although this chapter somewhat arbitrarily divides suggestions between the two rooms, many of the ideas can be borrowed from one room and applied to the other.

LEFT *A large utility sink makes hand washing delicate items easier. An attractive skirt, which matches the window curtains, hides cleaning supplies. Laundry soaps in good-looking containers are stored on nearby shelves for easy access.*

OPPOSITE *Cubbyhole-style open shelving simplifies sorting clean laundry and storing cleaning supplies. Using a front-loading washer and dryer allows a counter top for folding laundry. Nearby Metro metal shelves hold baskets for additional storage.*

The Laundry Room

Whether your laundry room is an ample area off the kitchen, a corner of the basement, or simply a closet-sized space near the bedrooms, it's the workhorse of the house. It should have practical storage systems but also look good. Doing the laundry is neither intellectually challenging nor aesthetically rewarding, but it can be made as pleasant as possible in a well organized, attractive space.

Cabinets. Cabinets are the major furnishings of a laundry room. Built in or freestanding, with the right choices you can make cabinets combine function and good looks. Evaluate your storage needs and then decide the look you'd like best. If you choose closed cabinets, look for ones with sliding doors to save space.

Appropriate cabinetry is not, however, limited to utilitarian styles. Remember that cabinets designed for other rooms can be adapted to laundry room use. The top half of an old pine hutch, for instance, could be mounted to the wall behind the washer and dryer units. The lower half could be placed against another wall and used as a folding area, with the drawers and cabinet space underneath providing storage. Choose from a wide variety of armoires and wardrobes, extra-deep bookshelves, and vintage wicker étagères. Any piece with shelf space or other storage capacity can work to make your laundry room attractive.

Also consider salvaged built-in cabinets and closets removed from old houses. These can be found at salvage yards and flea markets, and often need only a little cleaning and a fresh coat of paint. Paint the interior a different color from the exterior or line the shelves with striped or floral wallpaper to create a small visual treat when you reach for laundry supplies.

Tables. A laundry room needs a surface for folding and sorting. A round table in a big laundry room creates a great work surface. Consider a cast-off kitchen table painted white, or even better, yellow. An old folding rectangular table—the type used by caterers and wallpaper hangers—can be fitted with a fabric cover to provide a smooth place for folding laundry or act as a large ironing board. A small table and chair set up as a sewing area is handy for quick repairs to clothing and linens.

Containers. Baskets aren't the only containers that perform well in the laundry room, but they lead the list. Designate a basket for each family member's clean clothing so it's easier to sort and transport back to bedrooms. Keep a large flat basket with handles to carry sheets and towels to bedrooms and bathrooms in a single trip. Or use three identical deep baskets with lids as laundry hampers; label them by washing temperature: Hot, Medium, and Cold. Store cleaning supplies in a basket, making it simple to carry them to other rooms. If there are young children in the family, store this basket on a high shelf. Other containers that can add a dash of style to the laundry room while holding soap powders, fabric softener sheets, and other supplies include:

- French canning jars,

- Large ceramic cookie jars,

- Stainless steel canisters with glass lids,

- Clear plastic pantry containers with colored, snap-on lids,

- Vintage wood produce crates with original labels.

OPPOSITE *A hanging painted corner cabinet brings a dash of Old World charm to a clean-lined laundry room. A stacked washer and dryer leave enough room for cabinets with generously sized drawers. The step stool is a useful addition.*

Miscellaneous Additions. It's also helpful to have a rolling laundry cart fitted with a cloth bag, a step stool, a generous waste paper basket, and even a small television or stereo to help pass the time while you sort, fold, and iron. An attractive folding screen can hide a corner where you store brooms, mops, and the vacuum cleaner.

In a basement or second-floor laundry room, install a small refrigerator for snacks and drinks. That way you won't venture to the kitchen midway through the ironing and then conveniently forget to return. Sometimes being organized is a matter of being able to stay with an unappealing task.

SHELF HELP

Too often laundry room shelves are disaster areas, cluttered catchalls in drastic need of some sort of organizing system. Chief culprits are all the tattered and stained towels and sheets saved to serve as dust cloths and cleaning rags. No one who isn't washing the windows of an office building or dusting every room in a small hotel needs more than a medium-sized basket of cleaning rags. Choose a good-looking rectangular basket, fill it, and then throw away the excess.

Do-it-yourself shelf systems, like metal Metro shelves, offer a multitude of clever configurations, but even built-in, fixed shelves can be organized to suit your particular needs. Some suggestions:

- Open shelves located near the washer make spotting detergents and other laundry products fast and easy.

- Organize sheets by size and store each size on a different shelf.

- Put newly clean sheets and towels at the bottoms of the stack and always pull from the top. That way, your linens are rotated regularly.

- Roll towels like newspapers and place them in baskets that fit neatly on the shelves.

- Line shelves with labeled metal bins to hold miscellany like light bulbs, extension cords, and picture-hanging tools.

- To cheer your soul while you deal with soiled laundry, leave room on one shelf for a personal collection such as art pottery vases or colorful vintage water pitchers. Hanging a framed collage of vintage clothespins would add another charming touch.

OPPOSITE *Lined baskets prevent snagging of linens and are convenient to tote back to a bathroom, bedroom, or linen closet. A pistachio green wash on the baskets complements the laundry room's color scheme and softens the utilitarian nature of the space.*

A PLACE FOR CUBBYHOLES

Schoolhouse-style cubbyholes create instant organization in a laundry room or mud room. Buy them ready-built, build them yourself, or create them by setting wooden boxes on their sides. Stack cubbyhole-style boxes to create a well-organized pyramid, attach them to walls wherever space and need dictate, or set them on a tabletop, shelf, or under a counter or work surface. You'll find they have a myriad of uses.

Paint wood cubbies to match the wall or trim color of your laundry or mud room, or create a decorative kaleidoscope by painting them in a range of different hues. Be sure to use washable eggshell or semigloss paint.

In the laundry room, sort clean laundry into individually labeled cubbyholes and let each child put his own clean clothes away. (Metal bin labels look tidy and eliminate confusion.) Keep soaps, bleach, and stain removers in cubbyholes close to the washing machine. Use another for the iron and its extension cord.

In the mud room, store shoes, lunch boxes, backpacks, and books to be returned to the library in cubbyholes and eliminate frantic last-minute searches. Place a picnic basket filled with a folded cloth, paper plates, and plastic cutlery in its own cubby, and you can organize a picnic on short notice. Even the family pet deserves a cubbyhole to store grooming tools, medicine, and a sweater, raincoat, or just a soft towel for drying off after walks in wet weather. If you have a vacation home, reserve a cubby for items you want to take there.

Although square cubbyholes create a nice graphic look, consider also incorporating some rectangular sections similar to school lockers without doors. Place pegs in each section and label it with a family member's name. These aren't just for children. Adults can use them to store tennis rackets and hiking poles as well as coats, caps, and scarves.

OPPOSITE *Shaker-style pegs and a simple wood bench turn a back hall into a working mud room.*

Mud Rooms

New homes often include an old idea: the mud room, a transitional space between outside and inside where muddy boots, wet jackets, umbrellas, and the like can be shed and stored. Even if your home does not include a separate room adjoining the back door, you can equip a service porch or even a small back entryway as a functional and inviting mud room.

Moreover, modern mud rooms serve as convenient spaces for arranging flowers, wrapping gifts, and even washing the family pets. Available space will dictate how elaborately you can outfit your own mud room, but, at a minimum, you should include the following.

- A place to sit while removing wet, muddy, or snow-encrusted shoes or boots. A bench with storage space under the seat is ideal.

- A wood, metal, or plastic-coated shoe rack to keep footwear organized.

- Some sturdy hooks for hanging jackets, hats, and backpacks, plus a hook designated solely for keys.

- And, for a decorative touch in even the smallest space, a good-looking washable rug and a heavy doorstop to keep the door open while you haul groceries inside.

From there, space permitting, add:

- Cubbyholes of various sizes depending on your family's storage needs. Hang some low enough for young children to reach easily;

- A bulletin board or chalkboard for family reminders;

- A vintage wall-hung plate rack to hold mail.

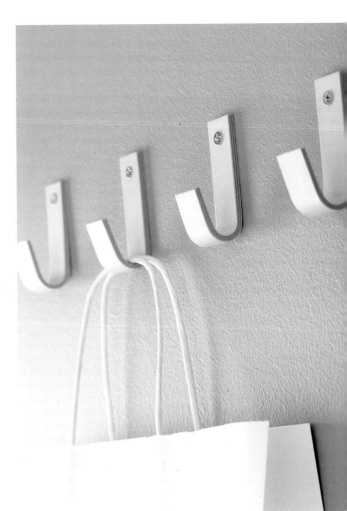

ABOVE *Wooden hooks can be mounted on a mudroom wall to handle family gear ranging from gym bags to dog leashes.*

OPPOSITE *Colorful paint for the walls and inexpensive, easy-to-install coat and shoe racks quickly organize a once-chaotic back entryway.*

The corner of a mud room becomes an eye-pleasing vignette without sacrificing its usefulness. Oversized schoolhouse-style hooks are as practical as they are attractive.

Pull-out units beneath a back staircase allow for organized storage of out-of-season shoes and boots.

If you're fortunate enough to have a real room to dedicate to mud room duty, here are some other useful additions:

- A large utility sink, with a towel bar or hook mounted nearby, and a large pump-style soap dispenser.

- An open basket near the door for dog leashes, balls, and other pet toys.

- A plain metal garbage can spray-painted fire engine red or pale periwinkle to hold dry dog food. Attach a metal scoop to the can's handle with a length of chain.

- A park bench with a distressed paint finish that will only look more interesting with heavy use.

- A long table created from a slab of wood laid across a pair of two-drawer file cabinets. Even an old door will do. The top makes a good place to set down grocery bags, packages, and back-packs, and the drawers provide yet another place for family files and records.

- A supply closet or set of oversized, floor-to-ceiling cubbyholes. If you shop for household supplies in bulk—from a case of toilet paper to multiple cases of cat food—a designated storage space just inside the back door is ideal. An added bonus: a quick glance on the way to the discount store reveals exactly which items need replenishing.

- A copper-lined wood bin for extra firewood.

FOCUSING ON FLOWER ARRANGING

Fresh flowers are an integral part of the stylish, organized home. And when clutter is under control, a myriad of surfaces are available to showcase them. Transforming blooms scooped up at the farmer's market, an oddly mixed bouquet from the grocery store, or cuttings from your own garden into simple arrangements is a quick, pleasant task when you have a designated work area with supplies right at hand.

Create a flower arranging station wherever you have a utility sink: in the mud room, laundry room, or even a corner of the garage. Start with some sort of work surface, perhaps an old kitchen table or a wooden workbench found at a flea market. A board laid across wooden saw-horses will work; use the space below for baskets and wooden crates to hold supplies. You'll also need shelves: either hung from the walls or as part of an old cabinet or hutch.

Then add:

- Nesting galvanized buckets, for transporting and conditioning flowers;

- An assortment of vases;

- Jars of clear marbles and small black rocks for anchoring flower stems;

- A large wastebasket;

- Clippers and scissors, organized into containers or hung from a pegboard;

- Commercial cut-flower preservative or, at least, some household bleach to add to vases to reduce bacteria;

- A spray bottle to mist houseplants;

- A small cutting board for whacking thick stems and branches;

- Sponges, whisk broom, and dustpan for cleanup;

- Dish soap and bottle brush for washing vases.

OPPOSITE *A deep sink and plenty of open shelf space make this corner of a mud room a functional flower arranging area. The rustic nature of the materials and accessories contribute to its charm.*

celebrating in the organized home

Celebrations are not just about big occasions—birthdays, anniversaries, and well-known holidays—but also about celebrating life's smaller pleasures. Invitations to "Come see my roses," "Come taste our homegrown tomatoes," or "Come celebrate the completion of our remodeling" are just as welcome as "Come have Thanksgiving dinner."

Celebrations are about spending special time with family and friends, but to enjoy these times to the fullest, you need to be organized.

Menu selection, food shopping, and table setting are important aspects of creating many memorable celebrations, but hostess gifts, imaginatively wrapped presents, and simplified, but stunning, holiday decor also deserve creative attention. Once some easy-to-execute groundwork is in place, preparing for celebrations both small and grand becomes more a pleasure than a chore.

OPPOSITE *With party essentials pre-selected and set out for a final check, setting the table can be accomplished quickly and stylishly.*

RIGHT *Extend celebrations to small pleasures, such as afternoon tea. Using your favorite china marks the moment as important.*

Party Planning

Whether you are having a sit-down dinner for eight or a Sunday brunch for eighteen, a bridal shower in the garden, or an Oscars-watching party in the family room, one basic rule applies: Start early.

For a dinner party, magazine articles repeatedly advise setting the table the night before. Good advice, but two nights ahead is even better. This gives you time to polish silver, find the extra wine glasses, iron napkins, or even rush a soiled tablecloth to the one-day drycleaner. Set out any serving dishes that will go on the table so you leave sufficient space for them.

Even a casual table setting benefits from being done ahead. Inevitably you discover that the straw placemats you'd planned to use look a bit tired or that several of the chunky Mexican wine glasses have chipped rims. By getting the linens, dishes, and glassware under control, you can enjoy creating the centerpiece the next day.

If you are incorporating even a small number of fresh flowers into your table decor, you'll find they look better having been arranged a day ahead. Supermarket flowers, in particular, open attractively in the warmth of the house.

Shop for nonperishable foods well ahead of time. Before Thanksgiving, for instance, you should grab the canned pumpkin as soon as it appears on the store shelf. Bags of cranberries can go into the freezer and keep perfectly for weeks. That jar of ground cloves you consider essential to your pumpkin pie should be bought early, not searched for frantically the day before the holiday.

Cook ahead as much as possible. Many, many dishes improve after sitting overnight in the refrigerator. Most guests would rather dine on a wonderful made-ahead stew served by a relaxed host than the finest filet mignons sautéed at the last, frantic moment.

ABOVE *Extend celebrations outdoors in warmer months. Change table and chair covers to suit the season and the occasion.*

OPPOSITE *Party favors set a festive mood for holiday entertaining. Keep the favors simple and the wrappings lavish.*

SEVEN SIMPLE CENTERPIECES

- Place an extra-lush pot of trailing ivy in a basket or cachepot. Tuck in florist's vials, and, in each one, place a flower.

- Instead of placing flowers in the center of the table, use a cluster of candles. Then place a bud vase with flowers at each place setting. If using place cards, tie them to the bud vases with slim ribbons.

- Arrange a low, full bouquet in a mason jar; then place the jar inside a tureen. The tureen will give the arrangement additional height and width, making it look more lavish.

- Pyramid glossy fresh vegetables such as shiny purple eggplants or large red peppers on top of a simple white cake plate. A few strategically placed toothpicks will stabilize the structure.

- For a children's party or baby shower, group toy chairs of different sizes in the center of the table and fill with a variety of teddy bears. Make small cones from brown wrapping paper or old grocery bags and tie miniature carnations or spray roses into an equal number of small bouquets. Just before guests arrive, insert the bouquets into the paper cones and slip them under the arms of the stuffed bears.

- Plant wheat grass in low metal troughs or shallow pans to give the table a cool contemporary feel.

- Buy several mixed bouquets from the grocery store and dismantle them, separating the flowers by color. Re-mass the blooms in small vases for a casual but festive look.

Setting a Special Table

Here are five ideas for festive table settings.

- Give new life to old napkin rings with a little gilding. Dull wood, tired brass, or outdated painted napkin rings can be transformed using copper, aluminum, or Dutch metal (fake gold) leaf from kits available at art supply stores.

- Start a collection of red, blue, or brown transferware. For parties, mix the pieces with plain white everyday plates. Using a basic plate, such as a white ironstone-style, with a more colorful piece, extends the usefulness of growing, yet incomplete, sets.

- Set dinner plates on solid color chargers in rich hues of green, gold, silver, or red to take place settings from ho-hum to knock-out. Red chargers, for instance, look terrific not only at Christmas, but also on Valentine's Day and the Fourth of July. Chargers also look good against the bare wood of a tabletop, eliminating the need for washing and ironing a tablecloth or placemats.

- Place a small gift at each guest's place setting. It need not be extravagant: a miniature box of chocolates, a package of unusual flower seeds, or even a small ornament will make each guest feel special.

- Accent your dining room chairs as you would a gift, with ribbons and bows. Tie a soft ribbon—organdy is particularly pretty—to the back of each chair and finish it off with a bow. Plan on two to three yards (1.8 to 2.7 m) of ribbon per chair. Instead of putting place cards on the table, tie gift tags with guests' names to the bows. For a bridal shower or birthday luncheon, tuck a small bouquet of flowers in the bow on the honoree's chair and a single bloom on each guest's chair.

ABOVE *Having a variety of unique vases in assorted sizes makes flower arranging split-second simple, whether using garden blooms or a grocer's mixed bouquet.*

celebrating in the organized home ❖ 145

Help from the Household Journal

Some simple jottings in your household journal will make organizing for celebrations easier.

- Record not only guests' food allergies and other dietary restrictions, but also the foods they most enjoy. Why bake a pie for someone whose idea of dessert heaven is homemade ice cream or peel potatoes for someone who prefers pasta? Gathering this information is easy. People talk about food in all kinds of situations; a note slipped into your pocket or purse at the time and then entered in your household journal will pay off later.

- Note table settings that work. Several months later you may have forgotten how terrific the amethyst wine glasses looked with the ice-blue placemats. When Christmas approaches, the memory may have faded of the previous year's easy centerpiece of lady apples and boxwood mounded in a silver bowl.

- Throughout the year, whenever you hear family and friends mention a favorite color, an admired author, a new hobby, or an appealing clothing style, write this information in your journal. These clues will help immensely at gift buying time.

OPPOSITE *Nothing says "celebrate" like a well chilled bottle of champagne. Keep crystal flutes on a silver serving tray for easy distribution.*

Hostess Gifts

- Never burden a busy host or hostess by arriving with a big bouquet of fresh flowers, no matter how beautifully encased in cellophane and ribbon. A few blossoms from your own garden, already arranged in a bud vase and thus easy to place on a tabletop or shelf, probably would please the party giver, but anything that requires vase hunting, arranging, and attendant fiddling is an imposition.

- An herb basket, on the other hand, looks charming and can be set right onto a kitchen counter. Fill a simple basket with a small sampling of potted herbs. Check specialty nurseries for unusual varieties such as pineapple sage, lemon thyme, and opal basil. If you're attending several parties within a short time period, buy an assortment of small baskets and a full flat of herbs. When about to leave for a party, you can grab a basket, drop in a couple of herb pots, tie a ribbon and gift card to the handle, and be off.

- Instead of a gift for the hostess, take small gifts for her children. Cleverly wrapped books or puzzles will please both parent and offspring.

- Since pets often are as treasured as children, make your hostess gift a treat for Fido or Whiskers. Drop a squeaky dog toy, catnip-stuffed felt mouse, or some organic pet treats into a small bag, tie shut with raffia, and be sure to include a tag indicating that the gift is for the pet and not the human members of the household.

- Stock up on small wooden spoons. Ones made from olive wood are particularly attractive. Using pretty ribbon to tie a spoon onto a jar of imported jam or gourmet mustard turns a pantry item into a party gift.

- Use fabric sacks to wrap bottles of wine. Paper wrapping never conforms to the bottle shape and decorative paper sacks often end up looking as if you just dashed into the local liquor store. If you have the time and even minimal sewing skills, make sacks from interesting fabric remnants, or stock up on ready-made versions when they go on sale. Fabric sacks also make a festive presentation for a bottle of fine olive oil or a container of home-made herb vinegar.

- The best tangible sign of appreciation, however, is a sincere and prompt thank-you note. Tangible is the operative word here. Not an e-mail or a phone call, but a handwritten note on attractive paper. This is incredibly easy to accomplish if you keep monogrammed correspondence cards and stamps in a handy location. Before leaving for the dinner party, birthday bash, cocktail buffet, or whatever, sit down and address the envelope to your hosts. Add a stamp and leave card and envelope out in plain sight. The next morning, write two or three lines expressing your appreciation and drop the card in the mail.

Gift Wrapping

Getting organized about gift wrapping is simple if you minimize the paper choices. With just three basic papers you can produce gorgeous gifts from New Year's Eve table favors right through a year of birthday presents, hostess and wedding gifts, and even the big holiday wrapping crush.

Start by investing in extra-large rolls of brown Kraft paper, a glossy-finish white paper, and a matte or shiny silver paper. Now, when you need to wrap a gift, you can forget last-minute shopping for the perfect paper and coordinating ribbon. Gone forever will be the maddening moment of opening a new roll of paper and discovering it's too skimpy to cover a large gift box.

Instead of amassing a hodgepodge of papers, build up a collection of interesting ribbons, raffias, skinny silk cords, and other pretty ties, which are more fun to shop for and far easier to store. Almost any that catch your fancy will work with one, if not all three, of the basic papers. Make another collection of small items to tie onto the packages. Nothing makes a package look more thoughtfully wrapped than a clever little topper.

For example:

- Wrap a Chinese cookbook in the brown Kraft paper tied with thin red silk cord and a pair of chopsticks.

- Use the silver paper, ribbon a color from the bride's kitchen, and a trio of different-sized whisks for a shower gift.

- Glossy white paper, wide grosgrain ribbon in pink, blue, or yellow, and a hand-knit baby cap tucked under the bow combine to make a baby shower gift look special.

- Commemorate a close friend's fiftieth birthday with the gift of a fine fountain pen. Wrap it with silver paper and wide black satin ribbon; then pin on a red silk dressmaker's rose.

- Brown Kraft paper and twine make a perfect wrap for a child's paint set. Tie extra paint brushes into the twine bow.

- Wrap holiday gifts in the glossy white paper tied with green satin ribbon and red Christmas tree balls. Or switch the colors to red ribbon and shiny green balls.

- Silver paper, gold ribbon, and small dried artichokes spray painted gold make a spectacular holiday wrap.

If you tire of one of the papers, substitute another—perhaps gold for the silver, or a red-and-white stripe for the plain white—but make it a true substitution and not an addition. Once you start expanding your papers beyond three or four colors, the ease of everything-goes-with-everything-else starts to diminish and the storage requirements start to grow.

ABOVE *Presents wrapped well ahead of time prevent pre-party panic. A convenient bench or tabletop holds them until time to go.*

Fresh and Simple Holiday Decor

Organize your holiday decorating by following two guide-lines: Keep it simple. Keep it fresh. By relying on fresh flowers, leaves, berries, and evergreens—augmented with ribbons and candles—you can create a festive look that's quick to set up and easy to dispose of when January arrives.

Begin by simplifying your outdoor decor. Let others spend countless hours stringing lights along gables or roofline and blanketing the foundation bushes with still more strands. Limit your lights to the area around the front door and a few trees in the front yard, particularly deciduous ones, whose trunks and bare limbs will appear sculptural when lit. As long as you have interior light showing through front-facing win-dows, your home will still look welcoming. Then, when the holidays are over, you'll not only spend less time taking down lights, but you'll need less storage space for them.

Instead of investing in an expensive fresh wreath, or a bulky-to-store dried one, for the front door, hang a flat-backed basket filled with fresh greenery. When you're expecting guests, add a few fresh flowers in individual florist's vials. As you put away the winter holiday trimmings, store the little vials in a small bag taped to the inside of the basket, ready for different looks throughout the year. Whatever the holiday, the principle stays the same: an inexpensive basketful of seasonal greenery, occasionally primped for company with the addition of a few blooms, ideally from your own garden.

Inside the front door, welcome guests with a simple but effective arrangement on a hall table. Scatter leaves on the tabletop and position four to eight apples, red or green, on top of the leaves as if they'd just fallen from a tree; turn some on their sides and keep others upright. Core three more apples just deep enough to hold taper candles. Keep the tapers under ten inches (25 cm) tall so they don't topple.

Make the powder room holiday-ready by turning it into a plant-filled winter garden. Stick to one bloom color, but be lavish with the number of plants. Group several on the floor in a corner and make another grouping on the sink counter. An array of white flowering plants, such as poinsettias, cyclamen, and paper-white narcissus works well in most powder rooms and looks terrific accented with silver ribbon. Coordinate the ribbon with any metallic fixtures: shiny silver ribbon with polished chrome faucets and a matte-finish rib-bon if fixtures are brushed nickel. When the holidays are over, move the plants outside to the garden or greenhouse and store the ribbon to use again.

Decorate the bedroom hallway by hanging a small wreath on each door. During the holidays, circles of fresh greenery, six to eight inches (15 to 20 cm) in diameter, are available at florist shops and even grocery stores. Measure the distance from the door top to the spot where you want the wreath to hang. Double this number to determine a length of narrow satin or grosgrain ribbon for each wreath. Loop the ribbon

and attach the two ends to the top edge of the door with a thumbtack. No need for bows or ornaments on these mini-wreaths; their style comes from their simplicity. Save the ribbons in a small, labeled bag, ready for another year.

In the family room, create a gift-wrapping center. Cover a game table or even a card table with a large fabric remnant in holiday colors. (No need to hem it; just cut the fabric long enough so you can tuck the edges under.) Store baskets of papers, ribbons, and tags underneath. When the wrapping is completed, leave the table up as a place to work on a holiday puzzle or play new board games.

And for a simple but charming decoration for the kitchen door, wire together a cluster of fir, pine, or cedar branches. Add a bow made from plaid or gingham ribbon or multiple strands of raffia, and tie on five or six holiday cookie cutters with more of the same ribbon or raffia.

buyer's guide

Resources for Creating an Organized Home

The suppliers listed here are just a sampling of the numerous companies that offer resources for creating an organized home. Many have worldwide distribution centers or international mail order via the Internet.

Architectural Salvage

Architectural Salvage Warehouse
53 Main Street
Burlington, VT 05401
802-658-5011
www.architecturalsalvagevt.com
Architectural salvage and used building materials

Discount Home Warehouse
1758 Empire Central
Dallas, TX 75235
214-631-2755
www.dhwsalvage.com
Architectural salvage

Bathroom

Waterworks
(Stores in USA and Canada)
800-899-6757
www.waterworks.com
Bathroom fittings and furniture

Containers and Organizing Supplies

The Container Store
888-266-8246
www.containerstore.com
Closet systems, storage containers, and useful organizing tools

Mariposa
Dealer locator: 800-788-1304
www.mariposa-gift.com
To the trade

Furnishings

ABC Carpet and Home
888 Broadway
New York, NY 10003
212-473-3000
www.abccarpetandhome.com
New and antique furniture and accessories

Anthropologie
201 W. Lancaster Avenue
Wayne, PA 19087
610-687-4141
www.anthropologie.com
Eclectic antiques and furnishings

Antique & Art Exchange
3419 Sacramento Street
San Francisco, CA 94118
415-567-4094
www.antiqueandartexchange.com
Interesting and eclectic collection of antiques and decorative accessories from around the world

Baker Furniture
Baker, Knapp & Tubbs
San Francisco Design Center - Showplace
Two Henry Adams
Suite 410
San Francisco, CA 94103
415-861-8866
www.kohlerinteriors.com
Stylish, well made furniture for every decor

Clark's Case
Hornsgatan 68
SE 118 21 Stockholm
Sweden
46-08-668-00-29
www.clarkscase.com
Contemporary furniture and accessories

The Conran Shop
55 Marylebone High Street
London, W1U 5HS
United Kingdom
44-20-7723-2223
www.conran.com
Essential pieces for a well-appointed home

Crate & Barrel
800- 996-9960
www.crateandbarrel.com
Furniture and accessories appealing to a variety of decorative tastes

Designers Guild
267-271 Kings Road
London SW3 5EN
United Kingdom
44-20-351-5775
www.designersguild.com
Colorful wallpaper, fabrics, and furniture by designer Tricia Guild

Gracious Home
1992 Broadway (at 67th Street)
New York, NY
800-338-7809
www.gracioushome.com
Screens, stools, storage systems, and other furnishings

Habitat
196 Tottenham Court
London W1P 9LD
United Kingdom
44-20-7631-3880
www.habitat.net
Furniture, housewares, and bed linens right
for a range of decorating styles

IKEA
www.ikea.com
Contemporary furniture with a wide appeal;
worldwide distribution

Imari
40 Filbert Avenue
Sausalitio, CA 94965
415-332-0245
www.imarigallery.com
Japanese screens, scrolls, art, and artifacts

Lassco
Mark Street (near Paul Street)
London EC2A 4ER
44-20-7749-9944
www.lassco.co.uk/antiques
Architectural antiques

Laura Ashley Ltd
P.O. Box 5
Newtown, POWYS 5IY6 1LX
United Kingdom
44-871-230-2301
www.lauraashley.com
Occasional furniture, wardrobes, linens,
and curtains

Leonards New England
600 Taunton Avenue
Seekonk, MA 02771
888-336-8585
www.leonardsdirect.com
Antique furniture, including a superb
collection of beds and accessories

Maine Cottage
207-846-1430
www.mainecottage.com
Painted wood furnishings

McGuire Furniture
Vermont Center
151 Vermont Street
San Francisco, CA 94103
415-986-0812
www.kohlerinteriors.com
Traditional and contemporary furniture
and accessories with classic appeal

Restoration Hardware
800-816-0901
www.restorationhardware.com
Furniture and accessories with a vintage style

Roche Bobois
585 Commercial Street
Boston, MA 02109
617-742-9611
www.roche-bobois.com
Coral Gables, Palm Beach,
Naples, Washington, DC
Traditional and contemporary furniture
with eclectic appeal

R.O.O.M.
Alstromergaten 20, Box 49024
SE-100 28 Stockholm
Sweden
46-8-692-50-00
www.room.se
Furnishings, closet organizers, and cabinets

Shaker Workshops
Arlington, MA
800-840-9121
www.shakerworkshops.com
Shaker furniture and accessories

Shibui
215b East Palace Avenue
Santa Fe, NM 87501
888-826-7849
www.shibui.com
Tansu and other Asian antiques

Spiegel
800-527-1577
www.spiegel.com
Furniture and accessories

Wisteria & Aptos Gardens
5870 Soquel Drive
Soquel, CA 95073
831-462-2900
Antiques, unusual containers, and fine plants

Paint and Finishes

Crayola Paints
800-344-0400
www.benjaminmoore.com
Washable and chalkboard paints

Farrow & Ball
888-511-1121
www.farrow-ball.com
Paint colors that are a departure from
the norm

Glidden
800-454-3336
www.glidden.com
Includes Ralph Lauren paints

ICI Paints North America
925 Euclid Avenue
Cleveland, OH 44115
www.icipaints.com
Wide variety of paint colors for every interior

Kelly Moore
www.kellymoore.com
Subtle and strong colors for interior and
exterior painting projects

The Old Fashioned Milk Paint Co.
436 Main Street
Groton, MA 01450
978-448-6336
www.milkpaint.com
Old-world colors and finishes

Storage Systems

California Closets
www.calclosets.com
Customized storage solutions;
worldwide distribution

photographer credits

Courtesy of Laura Ashley, Ltd., 5; 16; 27; 29; 82; 87; 96 (top); 141; 143; 145

Courtesy of Baker Furniture, 15 (top); 25; 30; 62; 78

Guillaume DeLaubier, 23; 47; 140; 159

Tria Giovan, 10; 32; 54; 66; 69; 84; 89; 92; 96 (bottom); 98 (left); 118; 142; 149; 153

Tria Giovan/Barry Dixon, Design, 46; 111

Tria Giovan/Phillip Sides, Design, 48

Courtesy of Glidden, an ICI Paint Company, 2; 6 (right); 21; 49; 51; 58; 59; 88; 103 (bottom); 105; 113; 117; 121; 125; 126; 128; 130; 136

Reto Guntli, 24

Courtesy of IKEA, 7 (right); 9; 53; 57; 79; 95; 101; 103 (top); 104; 107; 109; 116; 120; 134; 135

Courtesy of The Kohler Company, 98 (right); 99

John Edward Linden/Michael Sant, Architects, 73

John Edward Linden/Fernau & Hartman, Architects, 86

John Edward Linden/Ray Kappe, Architects, 81

Courtesy of Maine Cottage Furniture, 1; 67; 74

Courtesy of Mariposa, 146; 152

Courtesy of McGuire Furniture, 40; 65; 77

Courtesy of Roche Bobois, 6 (left); 36; 37; 43; 70; 112

Eric Roth, 15 (bottom); 28; 35; 39; 68; 115; 122; 133; 137

Eric Roth/Joni Davis, Design, 61

Eric Roth/Polly Peters, Design, 44

Eric Roth/Wendy Reynolds, Design, 83

Eric Roth/Debby Smith, Design, 108

Courtesy of Spiegel, 64; 91

Tim Street-Porter, 13

Brian Vanden Brink, 19; 50; 139; 156

Brian Vanden Brink, Elliott, Elliott, & Norelius Architecture, 127

Brian Vanden Brink, Mark Hutker & Associates, Architects, 20

David Weigle, 158 (top)

David Weigle/Randall Koll, Design, 150

about the authors

Randall Koll is an interior designer who writes and lectures on interior design and lifestyle-enhancing techniques. He is a regular contributor to the Home and Garden section of the *San Francisco Chronicle* and has been featured in such magazines as *Woman's Day, Good Housekeeping, B For Savvy Brides,* the *San Francisco Chronicle Magazine*, and *House Beautiful*. He lives in San Francisco.

Casey Ellis has written on design, art, and food for *House Beautiful, Good Housekeeping, Victoria*, and *Robb Report* and is a regular contributor to the *San Francisco Chronicle Magazine*. She splits her time between a 1910 house in Los Altos, California, and a 1937 William Wurster–designed beach house in Aptos, California, both of which have provided considerable source material—both comic and tragic—for her design writing.

acknowledgments

Our heartfelt appreciation goes out to the team at Rockport, and especially our editor, Mary Ann Hall, who supported our ideas from their earliest days. Thanks are also due to our excellent and patient photo editor, Betsy Gammons, who was always up for the challenge of finding the perfect photo to illustrate those ideas, and to project manager and copyeditor Josh Brackett, who shepherded the book to completion.